Our school – stories and memories

Bennett Road School Headingley 1882–2006

*More recently known as
Headingley Primary School

Bennett Road School Headingley 1882-2006

Headingley Primary School

Editor Mike Sells

Published in the UK by Headingley Network
2 Grove Lane, Headingley Leeds, LS6 2AP

www.headingley.org

© 2010, Mike Sells

Design dg3

Photographs as attributed

Print Kolorko, Bradford

All rights reserved. No part of this book may be reproduced, stored in a retrieval system, or transmitted in any form or by any means, electronic, mechanical, photocopying, recording, or otherwise without the prior written permission of the publisher.

ISBN 978-0-9567879-0-3

Contents

Introduction		3
Chapter 1	**The early history**	4
Chapter 2	**1920–1938**	14
Chapter 3	**1939–1945: The Second World War years**	24
Chapter 4	**1945–1952**	34
Chapter 5	**1953-1959**	40
Chapter 6	**1960–1990**	48
Chapter 7	**1990–2006**	56
Chapter 8	**HEART– a new era**	72
References and acknowledgements		74
Index		75

introduction

About this book

The idea of this booklet is to celebrate the life and history of Headingley Primary School (as it was known most recently) and also to mark its sad closure in 2006. We loved the school and wanted to capture something of people's memories and thoughts about it over its long history of 120 years.

In drawing all this together we have not aimed to create a precise and definitive piece of historical research – although we have tried to be as accurate as possible and to check out the facts wherever we could.

The earliest history is, of course, beyond the memory of anyone still living and so we have delved into some fascinating archives to try and bring that section to life.

After Chapter 1 the book is almost entirely made up of what people have said to us about their memories of their time at the school.

We are very grateful to the many people who have contributed to the booklet. We have received some lovely and intriguing accounts of 'how things were'. However limits on space mean that we could not include everything. We aim however to go on collecting material both in paper form and on the Headingley Network website. We hope that some of the paper material will be accessible in the school building – now 'HEART' (Headingley Enterprise and Arts Centre). We hope that people will be able to continue to add their own memories, stories or pictures.

Thanks

We are very grateful to Rachel Sannaee for nearly all of the work on the research and gathering together and editing the memories, stories and for most of the photography. Special thanks also to Eveleigh Bradford who researched and wrote the first chapter about the beginnings of the school. We are grateful to the West Yorkshire Archives in Leeds who gave us access to the oldest records, log books and plans. (See refs page 74).

Thanks are due to so many other people: to Lesley Jeffries for enthusiastic encouragement and advice; Joanne Shaw and Barbara Dane for work on the first collection of material; Joan Ramell (administrative support); Richard Crossley for looking after our accounts and Richard Honey for the design and printing of the booklet and the display.

We are very grateful to the Heritage Lottery Fund who provided most of the funding to make this possible. Thanks also to Martin Hamilton and the Headingley Councillors who also contributed funds, and to Headingley Network which has helped and supported the project in many ways, including making a loan to increase the print run.

The Film

We are also aiming to produce a short film about the history of the school! We are very grateful to Sean Stowell who has already made many hours worth of film which with his help, we intend to edit into a narrative about the school. Our intention is that this will also be available via the Headingley Network website www.headingley.org

Mike Sells

1 The early history

The school started life as the Headingley Board School, newly built in the heart of the village in 1882. Headingley then was a very different place from the crowded suburb we are familiar with today. There were still fields and gardens around the new school and old cottages scattered along the main road and North Lane. But this was a time of immense change. Industrialisation was continuing apace in the town and Leeds was full of 'industry and grime', smoke and squalor. The quiet rural village of Headingley, three miles away and 'up on the hill', had become a very attractive place to live and many of the early entrepreneurs had already moved here, building themselves imposing mansions and villas, many of which still survive. As conditions worsened in town, others were keen to follow.

HORSE-DRAWN TRAM ON OTLEY ROAD OUTSIDE THE WOODMAN PUBLIC HOUSE. COURTESY OF LEODIS WEBSITE

Public transport links were also developing quickly, making it possible for more people to choose to live in Headingley and commute each day to town. The main road connecting Headingley to Leeds – part of the original Leeds-Otley 'Turnpike Road' – was improved and in 1871 rails were laid for the very first horse-drawn tram service in Leeds, running from Boar Lane out to Headingley – faster and cheaper than the earlier horse-drawn buses. Later improvements, the introduction of steam power and finally overhead electric power, made daily travel even easier and contributed to a huge increase in Headingley's population from the 1870s onwards. It was seen as a healthy and desirable place to live, high above the industrial sprawl of the city, and the builders saw a profitable market for new housing. Close-packed terraces were quickly built, crowding over former fields and gardens. The new Board School was to provide a key service for all these new residents.

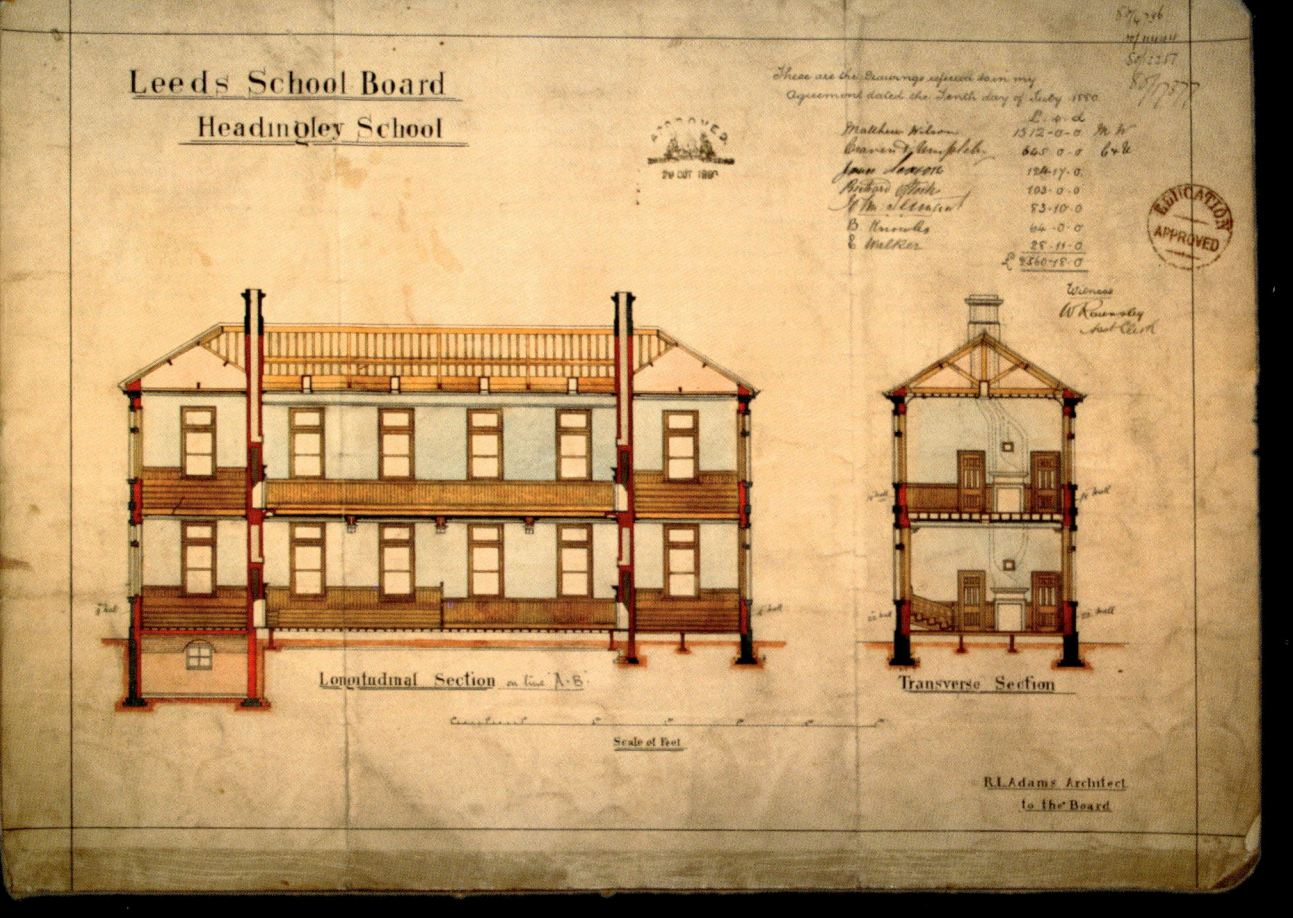

ORIGINAL ARCHITECT'S PLANS FOR THE SCHOOL 1880

The Site and Building

Under the 1870 Education Act, School Boards were set up across the country to ensure 'elementary' education was available for all children aged 3 to 13 (later 14). In Leeds the new Board faced a daunting task: more than half the 59,000 children in the borough were not provided for and an immediate and urgent programme of school building was needed. Attendance from age 5 to 10 was made compulsory for the first time in 1880, so enough school places had to be ready.

In Headingley there was already the large and well-run National School (St Michael's Church of England) as well as various private schools. However, as the population of Headingley began to expand it became clear that another school would be needed.

The site chosen was on a newly developed road, Bennett Road, where plots of land were being offered for sale by the Cardigan Estate. The road had been planned in the 1850s and the handsome Waterworks pumping station in North Lane (now 'The Taps' pub), which had opened in 1860, backed on to it. The rest of the road had remained mostly undeveloped and it was still bordered by fields and nursery gardens, but now the whole area was up for sale for building development.

By 1880 when the Board bought the site for the school (for £776), building had already begun along the road. Two terraces of houses had been built – Oak Terrace on the same side as the school, and South View Terrace opposite (both survive). Another plot of land close to the school site had been bought by St Michael's Church and plans made for a new Parochial Institute, with facilities for evening lectures, meetings, and a reading room opened – this finally opened in 1884 (now converted into offices). On the corner next to the school site were stables and outbuildings belonging to a grocer with a shop in the main road. Within a few years the land behind the school site was also being built over, as the streets and closely packed houses of the Granbys crowded round the school and its playground, enclosed within its high stone walls.

Before the school opened, the Board had to decide how to organise the intake, to take account of the existing National School. Policy at the time was to have separate boys', girls' and infants' departments and, maybe to save costs on the new school, the Board approached the trustees of the National School with the proposal that the National School should take boys only and the new Board School take girls and infants. The proposal was accepted and the new school was organised on this basis.

The building was designed by the Leeds School Board architect, Richard Adams. He was appointed in 1873 and was one of the most prolific Board School architects in the country. The Bennett Road School was built to the latest educational standards at a total cost of over £4,000. It was to be solid and spacious, without 'expensive ornamental features' both outside and in – a plain, handsome building, with an imposing entrance to the road.

LEFT: LOGBOOK – DETAILS OF OPENING 1882

RIGHT: ATTENDANCE LOG BOOK

It was planned to accommodate up to 333 children on two floors, with the infants downstairs and the girls upstairs. Each floor had a large central hall area, with a classroom on each side. Glazed partitions enabled the Headteacher to oversee what went on. The design reflected the Board's aim to provide well-planned teaching space, with good lighting and ventilation. Outside were two spacious playgrounds (physical exercise was viewed as important), partly covered for bad weather, with separate blocks of lavatories at the back.

The Board School opened on 10 July 1882 with 122 pupils; of these 58 girls and 27 infants had transferred from the National School (amid some grumbling), while the others were all new entrants – children who had never been to school before, with little idea of what to expect and, it was reported, 'no idea of discipline'.

Chapter 1 – Early history

Organisation and daily life

The two departments - the Infants' School, which was mixed boys and girls, and the Girls' School – operated quite separately, each with its own headteacher – Miss Boyle for the Infants, assisted by two pupil teachers, and Miss Dixon for the Girls, with the help of one pupil teacher. Each School had its own separate entrance, cloakroom, and walled playground.

The new school was regularly inspected by the Board's inspectors and visited by members of the Board, as well as by the Vicar of Headingley, perhaps keeping an eye on the religious instruction. The school had to follow the directions of the Board with regard to curriculum and discipline and the important issue of attendance (attendance figures affected the level of government grant). Until 1890 fees were charged – the school pence – but those who could not afford to pay could apply for relief. Attendance at school was not seen as important by all families, and children were often needed to care for younger siblings, or to help with chores, and so numbers fluctuated a great deal. Teachers would go and visit the home if pupils were absent more than a week.

INSPECTOR'S REPORT 1883

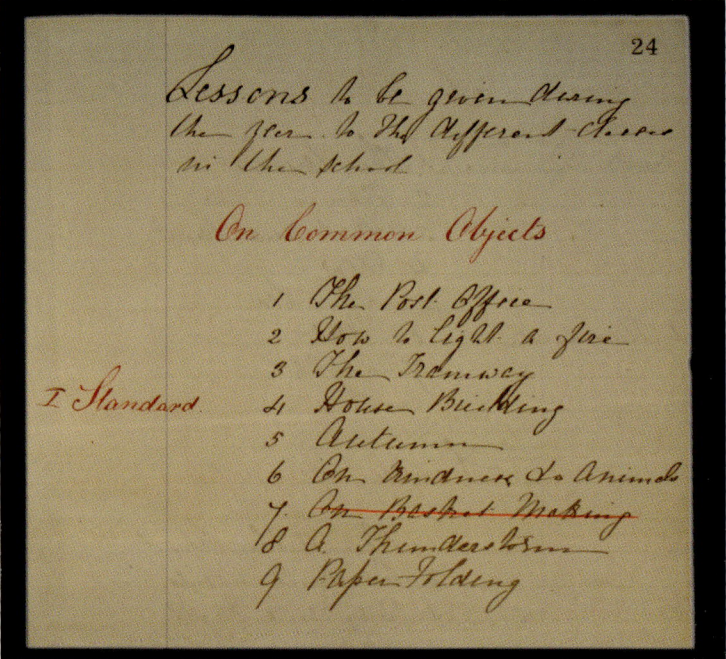

COMMON OBJECTS LIST

Our school – stories and memories of Bennett Road School, Headingley, 1882–2006

Attention to cleanliness was another concern: the teacher of the girls' school when it opened in 1882 noted that she had examined the girls for cleanliness and sent the dirty ones outside to wash! This kind of check was part of the opening routine of the day.

The Board inspectors sat in on lessons and reported on their progress, their comments all recorded in the School Log Books. The Log Books also contain careful notes on the children's lessons with much emphasis on reading, writing and arithmetic as required by the Board: a "thorough grounding" was viewed as essential.

Every day had to begin with a hymn and a prayer: religious instruction was compulsory but firmly non-denominational. Other subjects were supplementary but over the years were extended and enhanced. Needlework was viewed as particularly important for the girls of all ages; the school was occasionally criticised for not giving enough attention to needle-drill for the infants! Some lessons were based around one theme or article, see the illustration of 'Common Objects' on page 8.

The inspector examined the pupils over the age of 7 each year and much stress was laid on achievement (again the government grant depended upon successful results). The Infants' teacher noted in 1887 that several new older children had been admitted who were "backward", never having been to school before. Some children were recorded by the inspector as found to be "delicate, dull or backward" and were "not to be pressed".

The teachers themselves were also subject to rigorous inspection. The headteachers had to be certificated and were assisted by pupil teachers who were often only just above school age themselves (13 was the minimum age) and inexperienced. They did their job well, and overall the school received excellent reports from the inspectors – "a highly creditable state of efficiency" (1892)

Change and development – a mixed school

In 1893 there was a major reorganisation of the school. The Board had changed its policy on segregated departments, deciding that girls had 'a refining influence' on the boys and mixed departments were to be preferred. The previous arrangement with the National School was rescinded and

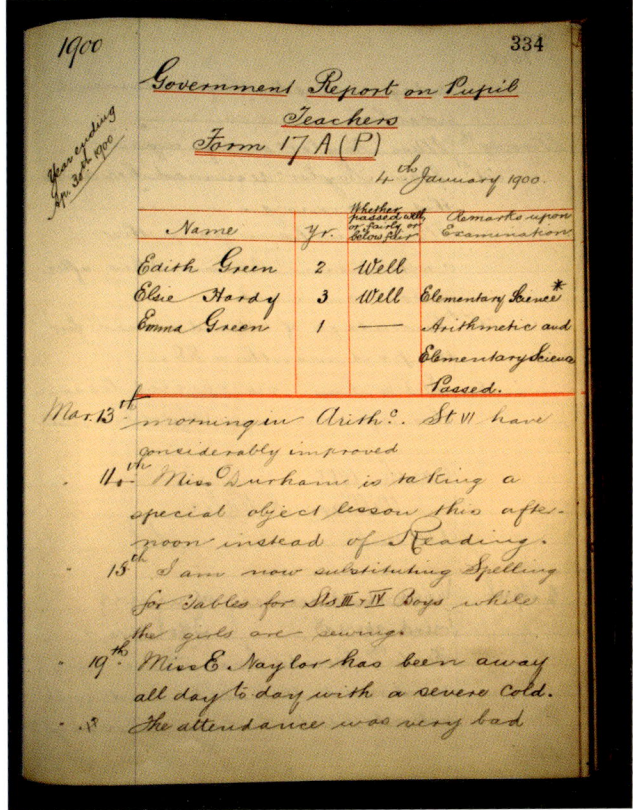

LOGBOOK 1896 INSPECTION REPORT ON PUPIL TEACHERS. THE PUPIL TEACHERS HERE WERE ABOUT 15 YEARS OLD.

Chapter 1 – Early history

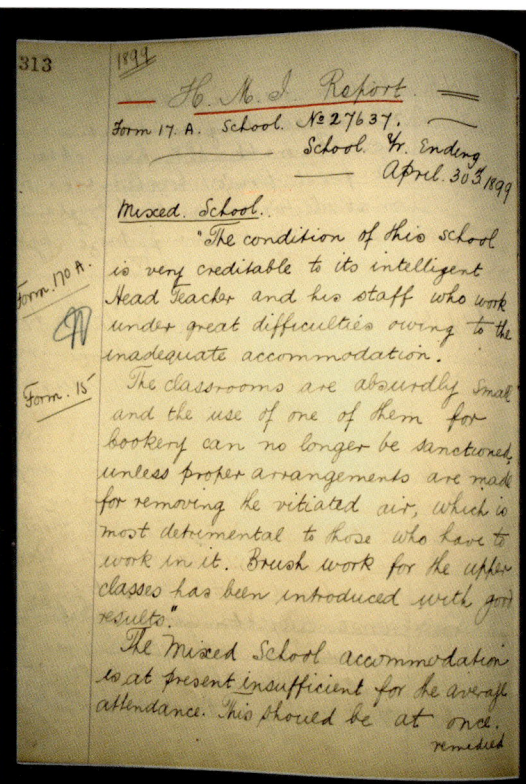

ABOVE: INSPECTION REPORT ABOUT OVERCROWDING

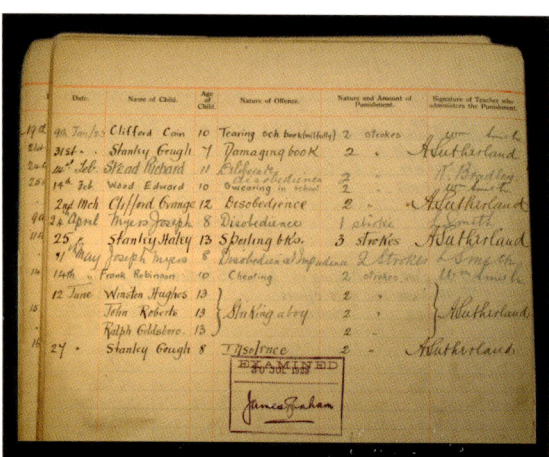

both schools reverted to being mixed. As the school was now taking older boys a new headmaster was appointed, at double the salary of the previous headmistress! While classes were mixed, boys and girls were still kept well apart when not under the teacher's eye, with separate entrances and playgrounds.

While numbers dropped at this point as some infants and girls transferred to the church school, they quickly built up again, as Headingley continued to grow, particularly with the development of the red brick housing in the Granbys, the Trelawns, the Manors, etc. By 1905 there were over 300 on roll and there was a problem of overcrowding which meant an extension had to be built (on the left as you look at the front). As it went right up to the boundary wall, an arched covered way was built through the new extension to provide access to the girls' and infants' playground and toilets at the back.

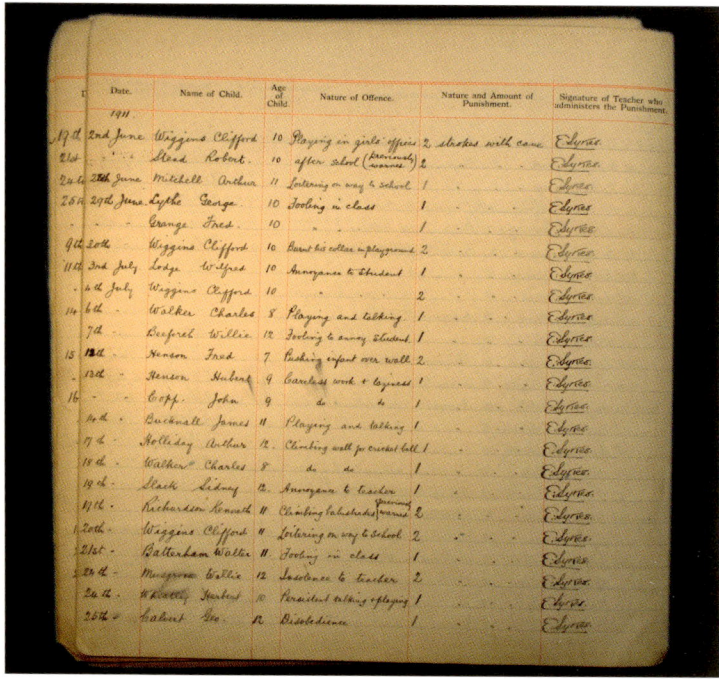

ABOVE AND LEFT: PUNISHMENT BOOK DETAILS

Our school – stories and memories of Bennett Road School, Headingley, 1882–2006

PUNISHMENT BOOK

Keeping order in the classroom

The classes were big and had to be strict. From 1905 any corporal punishment had to be recorded in a Punishment Book, which makes now for unsettling reading.

Many of the 'offences' seem to be fairly minor to current thinking. In 1905 entries in the Punishment Book included: "giving foolish answers in class to make class laugh" resulting in two strokes on the hand, "careless work in exercise book", two strokes on the hand, "insolent to teacher", one stroke on the hand.

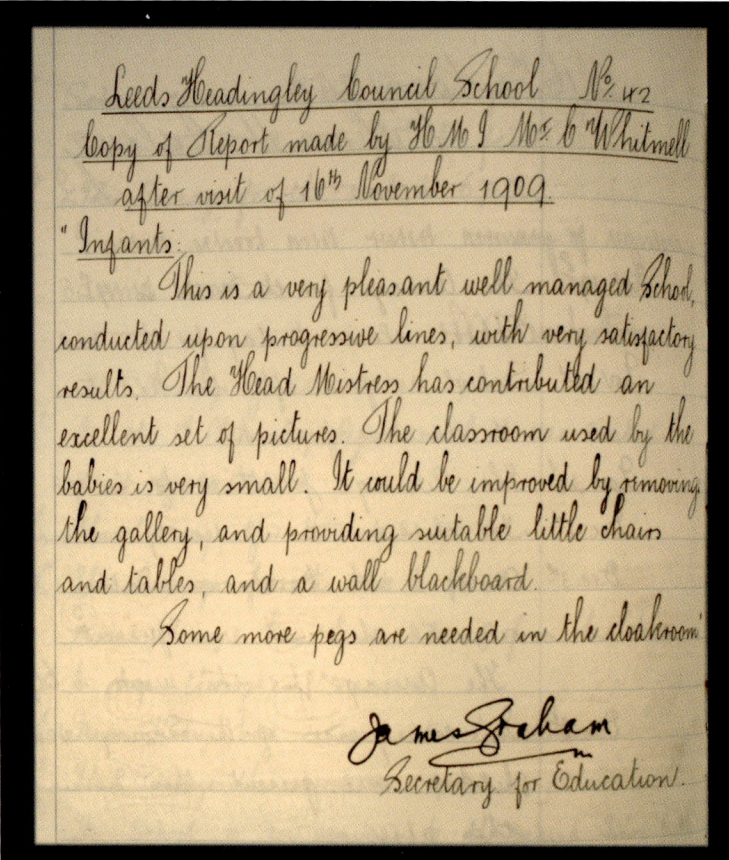

1909 INSPECTION REPORT.

A successful school

All the early reports indicate that this was thought to be a successful and efficient school, serving its children and parents well. For some years it also provided an additional educational service for the community as it housed the first free public library in Headingley, from 1884 until 1891, when a new library was built in North Lane.

The school provided many children with all the education they would ever receive and they left at 13 years. Only the select few went on to secondary education, and it is moving to see the pride and pleasure with which their achievement was recorded.

More pupils in the school

Headingley lost many of its men in the First World War, as the War Memorial outside St Michael's Church records, and many children in the school and their families must have been deeply affected. As the First World War ended, there was a national wish to improve the country's educational standards and in 1918 the school leaving age was raised to 14. This meant that Bennett Road School had to plan and accommodate an extra year of teaching for most of its pupils – although more secondary schools were to be provided, still only a small proportion of children went on beyond elementary level.

Bennett Road/Headingley Primary

A note on the name: following the 1902 Education Act, School Boards were replaced by County Education Committees, and as a result the Board School had its name changed to Headingley County School. After the 1944 Education Act, when secondary education was made compulsory, it became Headingley County Primary School, and then Headingley Primary School. However, its familiar name as long as anyone can remember has been Bennett Road School, and this is the name most people remember it by.

1904 CLASS PHOTO COURTESY OF LEODIS WEBSITE.

2   1920-1938

From this point on, the book switches styles as we rely on the accounts of people who were pupils at the school, in their own words. We are going back a long way so there may be some minor discrepancies in what is described – this is the furthest back we could reach with living memory!

The pupils attending Bennett Road during this period referred to the school as a 'through school' i.e. a child spend would all their school life in this school, from starting until leaving at 14 years old.

Contributors include: **Nellie Hopwood, George Barker, Edna Hepworth, Jack Tuffen, Delphine Maw, Arthur Staniland, Phil Smith and Ted Gaunt.**

The staff of this period, whom they recall, include:

Mr Cripps (Headteacher), Mr Morley (who lived in the Winstons), Mr Poll (who lived in Adel), Miss Calvert, Miss Bailey (younger children), Miss Kelly, Miss Ackroyd, Mr Lister, Mr Booth, Mr Dean, Miss Downing, Miss Gregson, Miss Pilling, Miss Cole, Miss Burrell, Miss Wilkinson and Mr Lightowler (Caretaker).

10 YEAR OLD'S CLASS, 1937.
THANKS TO A.STANILAND.

ADMISSIONS REGISTER 1925, (SEE ALL THE VERY LOCAL ADDRESSES)

School Organisation

"The school day was from 9 to 12 with an hour and a half for lunch, when we went home and returned for the afternoon session 1.30 to 4pm."

"Every morning when school started, we all had to line up and were ticked off on a register before coming in to the school building."

"Once coats were off, we assembled on the stairs first thing. There was no talking whilst we waited. We didn't have an assembly hall as such, but the big classrooms had sliding partitions and we opened them when a hall was needed."

"The Headteacher took assemblies for the whole school every day in the large upstairs room with hymns, prayers and readings. After this short assembly, we went to our separate classes."

"The young children were in the 'bottom part' of the school and the older children in the top classes were upstairs. I remember the infants downstairs had an afternoon sleep on raffia mats."

Chapter 2 – 1920-1938

"Around the back of the school there were two sheds where coke was kept and when the weather was bad, we could play round there under the shelter at the back of the building. The toilets were also around the back of the main school building."

"The building was two storeys high and only one classroom deep. It had a sort of 'tunnel' through the ground floor where a room had been missed out, the boys went round that side to get to the boys' toilets – they were outside of course. Also at the back was a covered area for 'wet weather PE'. Access to the girls' toilet was round the right hand end of the school."

"We all had to cross the playground to get to the toilets and there was a big one at the end for the teachers … you knew where they were going when they carried a very large key with them! "

"Bennett Road School was separated from the road by its high iron railings and concrete playgrounds, boys on the left and girls on the right. (There were iron railings at the front which were taken down during the 1939–45 war – ostensibly to make tanks.)"

EXERCISE BOOK – INSIDE BACK COVER 1934

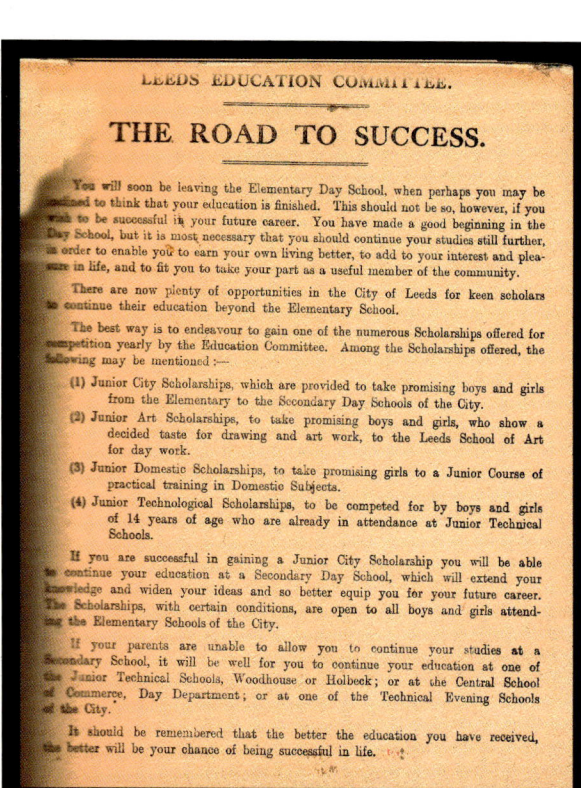

Classrooms and lessons

"In class, we worked as a whole class, spending a lot of time on Arithmetic, Literature and Reading. They were large classes with all the class doing the same work, at the same time, across the whole school day and sitting at the same desk (with ink wells) all the time. We all took it in turn to read aloud to the whole class."

"When we learnt to write, we started on slates with chalk and then moved on to using pencils and writing books, followed by pen and ink. This could be a stressful experience – it was a worry as I often was making messes with the ink and getting into trouble as a result. The worst thing about writing was pressing too hard on the pen nib which caused it to cross over itself and this meant a less than perfect result. Handwriting was emphasised greatly as was learning to write precisely using Waverley nib and ink."

"In between the classrooms, there were glass partitions (you could walk through from one to the next). The bottom part of the partitions were made of wood and pictures and maps were often stuck onto them. I remember there were open fires in the classrooms, which the caretaker stoked; the pipes were used to put wet clothes on to dry. There were rows of desks with fixed seats and inkwells in every desk".

"Cookery, for the girls only, was taken in a room at the side of the archway (this was later filled in to form a classroom) and dressmaking for the girls was held in the laundry on the ground floor of the school (at the right hand side as you look at the building). The boys did woodwork separately up at St. Michael's School."

Monitors

"The discipline was strict and lessons were in complete silence. There were lots of monitors who ensured there was no running, no talking on the stairs and in class they gave out items, collected and put things away. We had milk monitors who carried in the milk. Some saw the class monitors as the cleverest and they got the best jobs and gave out books and pens."

"Pupils had to queue on the steps and monitors enforced silence and neat lines of children. Monitors were appointed by the teachers and it was a role of importance; you had 'got somewhere' if you were chosen."

"We were encouraged to wear a blazer and school cap but this was not compulsory."

THE STAIRWAY – 120 YEARS OF WEAR

The playground

"The playground was used for team games like netball and rounders played in classes with the boys and girls separately. A low wall down the middle of the playground used to separate boys and girls but of course we jumped over it! Playtime was 15 minutes, morning and afternoon."

"Normally we played in the school playground with wickets drawn on the wall which separated us from Tasker's Garage but occasionally we went to Beckett's Park and played on the wickets prepared by the Municipal gardeners. In winter we played 'Touch and Pass' also at Beckett's Park – a child's version of Rugby League."

Off-site visits and trips

"The school netball team played other local schools. I remember catching the tram to get to a game. Sometimes there were trips to Beckett's Park for rounders but this was a boon, as it didn't happen often. There were regular trips to Blenheim baths and that was again on the tram."

"I remember once visiting Adel church for history and drawing it from the outside."

Chapter 2 – 1920-1938

"Mr Morley, the headteacher had an allotment at the top end of St. Anne's Road – possibly it was the school's – which we used and if we wanted, each child could have a patch to grow things in – it was something the older ones did after school."

POSTCARD FROM EARLY 1900S, CLEARLY SHOWING THE REMAINS OF THE ORIGINAL OAK ITSELF (FENCED OFF) IN FOREGROUND AND AN ELECTRIC TRAM. COURTESY LEODIS WEBSITE.

The headteacher

Bertha Calvert was clearly a headteacher who many people remembered very well. These are some of the comments:

"No nonsense, but she had everyone work hard and we should be grateful for her concern for us! ... Miss Calvert, a lady of great mana."

"... Tall, regal, and every inch a Headmistress ... Meeting her in the street one raised one's cap, said 'good morning Miss Calvert' and hoped to be rewarded with a smile! ... All rewards and punishments were her sole providence; the other teachers were confined to 'sending you to Miss Calvert'."

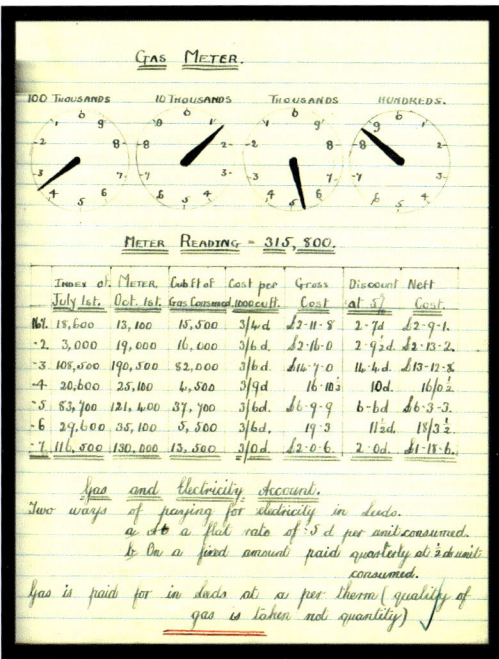

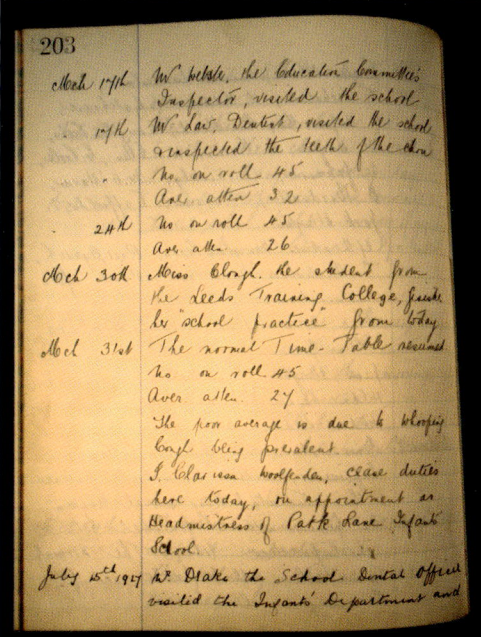

LEFT: EXERCISE BOOK 1934, SHOWING GAS METER CALCULATIONS

RIGHT: WHOOPING COUGH AND DENTIST VISIT 1927

MATHS EXERCISE BOOK 1934

Chapter 2 – 1920-1938

CLASS PHOTO 1926

Children's Day 1922–1963

Children's Day was one of the biggest festivals of youth staged anywhere in Britain. It ran for 41 years held each July and ran from 1922 – 63. It often suffered from downpours, which resulted in losses the volunteer organisers could not sustain. The organisers were the Leeds Schools Athletic Association and local businesses made donations with a group of teachers organising the day. Both the first and last Children's Days were washed out. A number of contributors have recalled attending and mention activities they were involved which are are described in later chapters.

CHILDREN'S DAY CERTIFICATE
1929

3 1939–1945: The Second World War years

This was a time period where we found that we had many contributors. The war years clearly made a very deep impression on the young pupils at school during that time.

At the start of the Second World War, in November 1939, the school closed for three months, like schools across the country, to construct its wartime plans. Air raid shelters had to be provided and plans for evacuation put into place, since the shelters would not accommodate all the children. In 1940 the school began registration of children to be evacuated to Burley-in-Wharfedale, where teaching and billeting arrangements had been made. As the war progressed, all kinds of special arrangements had to be put into place to ensure school life could continue and the children's education would not be too disrupted.

Contributors include: **Arthur Staniland, Sheila Heavisides, Ron Giles, Geoffrey Murdoch, Alan Cooper, Michael Westmoreland, Christine Richardson, Gwen Turner, Betty Carr, Brian Stevenson, Ralph Clark, Nina Boyce, Norman Schofield.**

The staff of this period recalled: **Bertha Calvert, (who continued as Head into this time period), Miss Matthews and Miss Day (headteachers). Miss Downing, Miss Gregson, Miss Bullimore, Miss Heal, Miss Pilling, Miss Cole, Miss Burrell, Miss Bloomfield.**

"Bertha Calvert, headteacher, was a patrician lady who inspired awe and fear in us, well remembered by pupils of the time for her slogan: 'Good, better, best never let it rest until your good is better and your better is best' and 'whatever is worth doing is worth doing well'."

The school building

"Whenever it was built, the elementary school I first attended aged 5 was already old and well established. Its stones were blackened, the school steps were worn, its desks well carved with generations of initials and tramways in the grain of the pine lids along which a generation or two must have slid their pens and pencils. Most of all I remember the old varnish on the panelled walls which afforded hours of inattentive fun flicking off hardened bubbles into which it had long dried.

Tall iron railings not only kept us in, and off the very busy but central Bennett Road, itself sandwiched between the steaming Headingley Laundry and Tasker's cindery garages, more importantly it separated the boys from the girls – each with their own entrance immutably inscribed overhead – and had been repeatedly painted green until one day the 'war effort' deprived us of our cages and the bars on which we happily swung."

"Essential 'plumbing' was outdoors – toilet facilities, such as they were, were open-air at the back of the building. Permission to use them being granted only after raising a hand in class and asking somewhat ambiguously 'please may I go round'. But we did have electric lights in Bennett Road, even if the caretaker living on-site did spend most of the day feeding the boilers with coke – when he wasn't filling inkwells in every desk from a long-spouted can, or deftly deploying saw dust where some unfortunate child had been sick."

THE ORIGINAL IRON GATE

"The playground seemed large with its dividing wall down the middle. At playtime there were games of skipping and 'tig'. The Institute (Parochial Church Hall) on Bennett Road was used for school activities including PE"

"At the back of the school there was a sheltered area where bikes were kept and sometimes PE took place there. On School Sports Day we went up to Beckett's Park and sometimes for PE lessons too."

'THE INSTITUTE' (THE PAROCHIAL CHURCH HALL) STILL THERE ON BENNETT ROAD – BUT NOW OFFICES

Chapter 3 – 1939-1945: The Second World War years

SLIDING CLASSROOM DIVIDERS – GLASS BOARDED OVER IN THIS PHOTO.

"The school day was 9am–12pm and 1.30–4pm. The youngest classes were across the bottom of the school building and the partition, which divided classes, was opened for assemblies and prayers first thing every morning."

"In the right hand entrance were cloakrooms behind grids. The stone staircase led up to another 'gridded' cloakroom and the headteacher's cosy room with its open fire. On the left hand school entrance was the needlework room, another staircase with railings led to the first floor."

"The first floor partition was pushed back for singing lessons and school assembly. Another classroom on the first floor was tiered rather like a lecture hall – we loved that room. There was also yet another enclosed cloakroom."

Swimming

"In our final year we went to learn to swim in the rather dilapidated shallow pool under the old Blenheim School. It took place every Friday at Blenheim School. The pool was grotty, very small and seemed to us to be in a cellar. The top two classes attended and you had to be good all week to go. This rule was applied very strictly. We used the tram from North Lane down to Notre Dame and from there would walk to Blenheim. The fare was 1d or 1/2d if we went half the distance and walked half the way."

"Anyway swimming facilities at least were available only a tram ride away in the Stygian depths of the frighteningly big (and also long gone) Blenheim School of which many were afeared and where I managed to earn a couple of ribbons to sew on my 'cozzy' but I'm grateful it was encouraged at such an early age. Like blue, silver, and exceptionally, gold stars, there always seemed to be something to win for something or other, and the ultimate acclaim – having one's name read out in assembly".

Responsibilities

"… there were monitors for everything. mid-morning, milk monitors distributed small bottles (1/3 pint) into which we all pushed (real) straws, through a little hole in the waxed cardboard lid and vied with each other to see who could make the loudest sucking noises."

"The large sash windows were opened and closed by window pole monitors – alas, I only aspired to stairs monitor, to ensure that ascending and descending was done in orderly single file, or be reported."

"I was promoted to be an 'ink monitor' and with my friend we both became 'door' and 'staircase monitors' to make sure pupils walked in single file up and down the staircase."

"Ink Monitors filled the two children's inkwells on each desk from a large stone jar. Register monitors took the register to the headteacher."

ELECTRIC TRAM ON ITS WAY FROM LEEDS ON ROUTE 'NUMBER 1' TO HEADINGLEY

Children's day

"Maypole dancing was enjoyed enormously and was also part of the Children's Day in which all Leeds Schools participated. It was held annually in Roundhay Park and six maypoles were laid out on the cricket field. Parents would take trams to the park to watch, there were queues of parents waiting to get on the trams. It was a wonderful social event, families took picnics, there were races, games etc.

The Handwriting Competition was held once a year and pupils had to copy out their 'best' handwriting. It was held in conjunction with Children's Day." (See certificate page 21)

CHILDREN'S DAY AT ROUNDHAY
PARK CIRCA 1930'S
COURTESY LEODIS WEBSITE.

Playground games

"We had very limited space but me managed to play rounders by the side of the school near the caretaker's house. There were always in season games – whip and top, conkers, skipping with endless songs and rhymes. We looked forward to playtimes when the Headingley Steam Laundry, next to the school, let off massive clouds of white steam. It totally shrouded the playground. No health and safety in those days!"

"The snowy season unfailingly brought slides and sledging. In the boys' yard at least, slide-life was extended with candle grease (but no hob-nail boots allowed). Conkers came and went leaving the yard littered with shattered ones, and the air ringing with such childish yells as 'fussie plank', 'na drags', 'na tibs', 'na strings'. So did whips and tops, hop-scotch and skipping, accompanied by weird chants mostly emanating from the girls' yard."

Bennett Road

"Further along Bennett Road was the Institute, accommodating the St.Michael's Cubs and Brownies, Sunday School, Youth Club, Beetle and Whist Drives and the British Legion (occasional dances featured their little band called the 'Legionnaires') to be resumed after its temporary occupation by khaki clad conscripts over which I clearly remember a tearful young Miss Todd (Standard 1V), peeping through a hole in the curtain-stuff above juvenile head height exclaiming 'but they are only boys!'."

BENNETT ROAD IN THE 1930S.
COURTESY LEODIS WEBSITE.

Chapter 3 – 1939-1945: The Second World War years

The sweet shop

"Peter Withey's kindly and white-haired old Mum had the sweet shop opposite the school (they lived next door), the tuck shop, full of glass jars, the ha'penny and penny boxes and the overall smell of liquorice in all its shapes and sizes – Pontefract cakes, Allsorts, liquorice shoe-laces, chewy root and a thick, round stick with a flattened end which blackened the teeth and lips in seconds. Lucky bags, lemonade crystals, aniseed balls, jelly babies, dolly mixtures, bulls-eyes and gob-stobbers (which we had to spit out into the wastepaper basket in class, usually just as we'd peeped at them changing colour) – none of your grown-up stuff in fancy boxes or cartons, but all served up in paper cones in exchange for the smallest denomination of coins. A post card stamp cost 1/2d which would get you a long way, into a cinema matinee, buy you a catapult or a packet of chewing gum out of a machine."

Classroom life

"The teachers sat on high stools at a very high desk with a good view of a large class of 48 children. The wooden dual children's desks had iron runners screwed to the wooden planked floor. The dual wooden seats tipped up on hinges, it was impossible to move. Some of the desks had 12 squared grids on the surface and all had small inkwells and a groove to hold a pen and pencil.

Every room had a blackboard – some were free standing and swivelled – plain on one side and red lined on the other. The high classroom windows made it impossible for a child to see outside the room."

THE CANE. THIS HAD BEEN KEPT BY THE SCHOOL, ALTHOUGH NOT USED FOR MANY YEARS!

The cane

"One hot summer afternoon I remember a very naughty 9 year old boy had to sit cross-legged in front of the teacher's desk. The rest of the class sat, arms folded waiting for a cane to be fetched from St. Michael's C of E School. I never remember the cane being used but it was a salutary warning."

School subjects studied

Poetry – "Four or five poems were learnt by heart each term. At the end of the term the headteacher would "test" us by calling at random on a child to come to the front of the class. We then had to recite the poem of her choice and were marked out of 10. The headteacher entered the marks into a very large official looking book!"

Nature Study – "Every Monday morning children took flowers for the classrooms. These were put in jars on the high window – sills. We had an 'annual trip', on a Monday morning, to see the bluebells in Batcliffe Woods. This was our only school outing."

Painting Lesson – "This was a laborious business! Large trestle tables were put in front of the class. Very large pots containing powder paint were set out in a row. In front of these pots were rows of 1 lb jam jars each with powder paint, which had to be refilled, by the teacher, from the large pots. Because of lack of desk space our painting paper was small and because of the number of children we had to put our hand up to ask permission to change our colour pot. To paint sea and sky by the end of lesson was an achievement!"

Composition – "We were given a title the week before and could write the composition at home. This was copied (painstaking work) with a very thin nibbed pen, into our composition book in class".

Arithmetic – "This was the basic 4 rules and endless repetitive learning of tables – to 12 times. Occasionally we had 'ruler drawing' lessons comprising measuring with a ruler and making designs".

Singing – "I can't remember what we sang but I can remember the teacher putting her ear to my mouth to hear if I was singing in tune ... I was never given the result!"

Practical skills – "Miss Grant took cookery classes with the girls in a dimly remembered and well appointed kitchen being better catered for than boys struggling with woodwork at their desks – but the smells were tantalising. Nevertheless, boys were encouraged to knit and sew – probably because as soldiers and so forth we'd soon have to anyway, and I duly embarked on a scarf in RAF blue."

Needlework – "About the age of 9 we all made large cotton bags. If the stitching wasn't perfect the teacher pulled it out and we had to do it again. We had to embroider our names in chain stitch and work a picture of our own design on the front (the robin on a twig on my bag was almost unrecognisable; however the cotton bag material must have been top quality as it is still in use 65 years later!). One special lesson our mothers visited to see our bags! We then embarked on 'door' rug making – marginally more successful than the cotton bags."

Story time – "Most of the stories told to us were much too complicated and adult – especially if you missed a few chapters through absence – however I still remember: Jason and the Golden Fleece; Alice in Wonderland; Christmas Carol; Greek Myths and Legends."

Games – "Rounders was played in the playground and when we were older we went by tram to Hyde Park and walked up to the Bedford Field playing field."

Other memories

"Plasticine came into my life in junior 1, making sand trays to illustrate Geography, History and stories we read. We did sums, we read and we had nature walks out on 'the ridge'.

Every Monday morning children took a penny and their small Yorkshire Penny Bank Book. The teacher collected the money and entered it into the small book and then into a large bank ledger. It seemed to take ages especially when children had to draw money out! During this time we had to learn part of a psalm and were 'tested' when the banking was completed."

The dentist visits

"Somehow, the heady enduring 'atmosphere' of Bennett Road School owed much to the all-pervading smells, the most fearful of which emanated from the headmistress's study when the visiting dentist was installed there periodically. Antiseptic, disinfectant, whatever it was, a vision of green screens, the tinkle of stainless instruments in white enamelled kidney dishes struck horror in the hearts of generations."

Travel

"I got the tram up Cardigan Road from the Beechwoods costing 1/2d. In the one and a half hour lunchtime I was able to get home and back to school.

Our class (48 children) decided as we got off the tram, from the sports field, that we would all step, in turn, on the conductor's bell. This was on the wooden tram platform. We were in trouble!"

TOP: DOORWAY DETAIL

BOTTOM: PANEL DOOR

The impact of the War

"… missing the infants class where 'babies' slept in rows under the watchful eye of Miss Pilling, I straightway entered Miss Cole's class or Standard I. The war was still two years off, when the school windows had a sort of net curtain glued to them, as did the trams which clattered along the Otley Road, only yards away."

"I recall the horrid smell of glue when men came to stick protective netting all over the school windows. The cold in winter when fuel for heating the boiler was in short supply. The eventual shortage of paper of paper, pencils and even pen-nibs. The visits of the school nurse and doctor to check not only for 'nits' in the hair but also general health of the pupils because we were restricted to a ration of food throughout the war and several years after."

"Netting was glued onto the windows to stop them shattering should the area be bombed; the school was later closed down for a period when evacuation occurred.
I remember in the period before Bennett Road reopened, a teaching group was held in St. Michael's Church, every morning for a few weeks."

"As for gas, passing through the mobile tear-gas chamber parked in the playground to test our gas-masks from which we were soon to become inseparable was mere child's play – though a few of more nervous disposition fainted, as they did when we were herded into the sand-bagged archway under the school during air-raid practice."

"The return of the Dunkirk veterans – they were lying down in the streets around the cricket ground."

"A lasting memory is going home from Bennett Road Council School one warm June afternoon 1940 and seeing countless soldiers lying on the roads and footpaths – they were dirty and exhausted having been rescued from the beaches of Dunkirk. They were billeted in Headingley homes. The following day we all compared 'souvenirs' mostly French coins, which the soldiers had given us."

"Going home from school one day, slumped exhaustedly along the cricket field wall (Kirkstall Lane end) were scores of war-weary soldiers still stained from the field of battle and the legendary evacuation of the Dunkirk beaches."

"We had to do our 'drill' in the playground because the war came and the 'institute' (Parochial Church Hall) was taken over as a reception place for the soldiers who were billeted in Headingley and who had commandeered the cricket and rugby grounds and the buildings there."

"If there was an air raid on our way to and from school we were told to judge whether we should run to school or home! This happened one lunchtime – there were no school meals, everyone went home at noon and returned for afternoon school at 1.30 – and we all ran back to school to take cover in the air raid shelter. The school air raid shelter was the passage way at the side of the school (later converted into a classroom), which was blocked at both ends by sandbags etc. There was no seating."

"Gas masks had to be worn at all times. These were carried in issued cardboard boxes, with a long string to go over your shoulders. We didn't go to school the day after bombs fell in Beckett's Park – instead I went, with friends to 'inspect' the craters."

"I do remember the air raids. The Germans had spoiled our sledging track in Beckett's Park, ruining the bumps at the bottom of the track that ran as far as the beck that used to freeze over. Beckett's Park played a large part in one's life – climbing trees, learning how to pitch a tent, baking potatoes in a fire: what freedom we had! "

"I devoured books in school but also spent hours in Bennett Road public library on the corner of North Lane; during the war books were scarce and expensive."

"Burley-in-Wharfedale was where many of Bennett Road's young schoolchildren were evacuated to. I was in Miss Downing's class at the time, Standard II. She and one or two other teachers accompanying us in neighbouring Mr Tasker's smokey old bus (from the garage adjacent to the school), complete with gas masks and labels. Yet less than ten miles distant, town and country were so utterly different in those more distant days."

LOG BOOK WITH RECORD OF EVACUATION 1939

LOG BOOK – PUPILS LEAVING 1940 – SOME AS EVACUEES

"Some were homesick of course, soon to be restored to the perils of Hitler's bombs and the wailing air-raid sirens which had us diving into our hastily dug Anderson shelters (if they hadn't filled with water) or under our Morrison tables."

"Some ten of us, boys and girls, were accommodated in a very large house in Burley - in - Wharfedale, the girls had one attic room, the boys another. We drifted back to Leeds, in my case evacuation lasted one day and night; a part time school was held in St. Michael's Church until Bennett Road re-opened."

LOG BOOK MAY 8TH 1945. SCHOOL CLOSED FOR TWO DAYS – VICTORY IN EUROPE.

Chapter 3 - 1939-1945: The Second World War years

33

4   1945-52

At the end of the Second World War the 1944 Education Act introduced immense changes to the education system. The school leaving age was raised to 15 and for the first time secondary education from age 11 was made available for all children, in different kinds of secondary school, determined by the '11+' examination. Elementary schools like Bennett Road were now termed primary schools, and took children only up to age 11, when they had to endure the painful process of selection.

Contributors include, include: **Eileen Pearsall, Val Dooks, Eric Blakey, David Lloyd Hughes, Margaret Ripley, Pat Pearson, Rosemary Boyle.**

Staff recalled: **Mr Pepper, Miss Matthews, Miss Day (headteachers), Miss Pearsall, Mr Sinclair, Mrs Nelson, Mr Mahoney, Mrs Townson, Mr McCann, Miss Downing, Miss Thomson, Miss Bronwich, Miss Burrell, Miss Johnson, Mrs Staton, and Mr. Longstaff (caretaker).**

The school buildings

"I remember there were two classes downstairs and the left hand cloakroom had a cosy open fire – the staff used the room at lunchtime, as there was no staff room as such. The classroom to the right was divided by a partition where the two infant classes were, it was opened up when we needed a hall."

"The outside toilets at the back of the school ... the urinals were made of slate or some similar black substance. This meant that anything liquid on them was very clearly visible. We had competitions to see who could raise the highest fountain on the black background!"

"Girls and boys were separated for needlework and mechanical drawing. The Parochial Institute was used for girls PE and the boys in the school playground or sometimes we used South Parade Baptist Church Hall."

OPPOSITE: DETAILS OF AIRVENT, RADIATOR AND DOOR HANDLE

Chapter 4 – 1945-52

1947 CLASS PHOTO

The school day

"We had one and a half hours for lunch and most of us went home. However in 1944 school dinners started being served direct from large metal containers. In the hall there were three long tables of children and I remember the teachers all had tall chairs so they could see over the children and watch what was going on."

"There seemed to be fairly lax security and many of us wandered about at lunchtime. I went a lot to the library and we all bought Horlicks tablets and liquorice root from the chemist, and apples and pikelets from the shops opposite."

The 11+ exam

"In those days we still had the 11+ and the day the results came out Mr Pepper (Head) came into the classroom to read out names of those who had passed ... later I realised it must have been very hard for those who had not passed to hear in that way but that is how life was in those days. We even had a photo taken of those who passed."

Cricket and sports

"The school had quite a good cricket team. We played in Beckett's Park usually on a concrete wicket. We had an odd collection of bats, some full size with the bottom 6inches sawn off. Our main rivals were St.Michael's. Mr McCann took our team to various Primary schools in north Leeds and we always travelled by tram. For gym St.Michael's school used the Institute on Bennett Road and in winter when there was plenty of snow, they were subjected to a barrage of snowballs if they passed our playground at playtime!"

"The Gray Trophy was an annual Leeds Schools competition; the school entered a team doing indoor athletics activities eg. high jump."

Culture

"Mr Pepper (headteacher) was very fluent in French and organised school trips for the top two classes to France. This was unusual for the time but continued over a number of years. There was a base for the trips at a school in St. Pol."

"I remember practising a play to be put on at 'The Institute' just along the road; we also went there to practise for the Gray Trophy and for country dancing for Children's Day."

FRENCH TRIP IN THE 50S
POSTCARD AND PHOTO.
THANKS TO M.RIPLEY.

Other individual memories

"Miss Matthews (Head) lived locally and to a five year old she appeared to be a lady of substantial proportions. I remember her well as one playtime I fell and gashed my head rather badly. A caring Miss Matthews gathered me up in her arms and carried me to the number 1 tram stop in Otley Road, taking me to the dispensary, where I had to have quite a few stitches."

"My friends and I had a bright idea of making money by putting a half penny on the Otley Road tram line in expectation that the trams iron wheels would press it into a penny."

"We lived in the Spennithornes (beyond the Ring Road), I recall getting the tram by myself at Otley Old Road and paying a ha'penny to Headingley. I had instructions to cross the main road at Bennett Road under the care of P.C. Rigton, who lived opposite us and whose two daughters also went to school."

"Whilst Miss Day was head the school changed its name to 'Headingley County Primary'."

BOOK PLATE

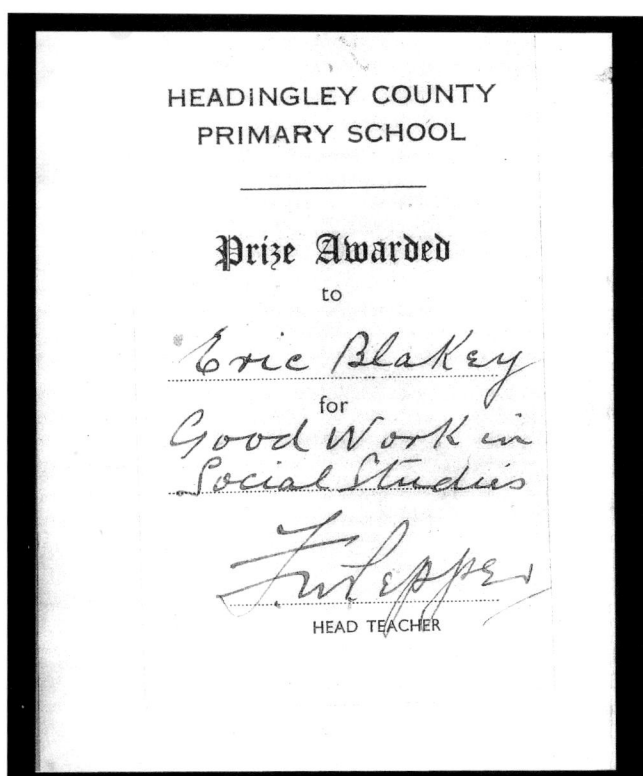

FRENCH TRIP GROUP FROM THE 50S

5   1953–1959

CLASS PHOTO 1956

The school seems to have settled into a steady period by this post war time with good attendance being the norm and the curriculum becoming much closer to that of today. There was however opportunity and encouragement for sports, music and other activities.

Contributors include: **George Sidebottom, Rachel Barton, Lynn Bairstow, John Simmonds, Gary Garabedian, Paddie Breeze, Martin Kettle, Robert Taylor, Rosemary Boyce, Jean and Paul Riley and Jacqueline Tuffen.**

Staff recalled: **Mr Pepper, Mr Hallet (Headteachers), Mr Sinclair, Mrs Shuttleworth, Mr Coultas and Mr Bainbridge (Caretaker).**

The school day

"We went to the Parochial Institute for school assembly, which didn't happen every day. The Institute was the next building along the road and we had to walk in crocodile past Headingley Laundry with its exotic aromas."

"I did not stay to lunch. I used to walk home and back and if my mother was not going to be home (not very often) I was given 1/6d as a treat for fish and chips which I got from the chip shop just by St.Michael's church and ate them at home with my grandma."

"Occasionally part of an afternoon was taken up with older classes enjoying singing traditional folk songs such as 'We jolly sailor boys', 'Lincolnshire poacher' and 'John Peel'."

"I remember now the sound of the hand-rung bell ... this was either welcome or not, depending on the time of day!"

"The milkman delivered the school milk to around the back of the school and if you were milk monitor you had to bring it in. In winter we put it by a radiator to thaw out!"

"Corporal punishment was accepted as part of everyday school life. One teacher would occasionally administer the cane on the palm of the hand at the front of the class."

RUGBY TEAM, EARLY 1960S

Rugby League

"Our greatest achievement at Headingley was representing the school in Rugby League. In our final year there we won the Regional Cup Final for our age group and to commemorate this occasion we were paraded in front of the entire school assembly."

"Mr Pepper and Mr Sinclair took the boys to Wembley one year to see the Rugby League Cup Final. We went by on the train very early morning and before the match they took us to see the sights of London."

Hobbies competition

"Another of my memories was the annual Hobbies Competition. This event was looked forward to by many, as it was an opportunity to show skill in areas that were not generally demonstrated in our daily lessons ... my entry was a pair of yellow gloves knitted using four needles! In the juniors we were often reminded to have interesting hobbies to keep us out of mischief when we were not in school. The annual hobbies competition was held so that we could produce tangible evidence of our productive lives to inspire other children and to impress our teachers and parents.

Every autumn term dividing screens between classrooms were folded back and sugar paper-covered desks were arranged around each classroom to form accessible display surfaces for the colourful collection of paintings and drawing, craftwork of all kinds, home cooking, knitted and sewn articles that were proudly entered for the prestigious competition.

Every child was expected to contribute and winners in each class could choose a book as prize. Most importantly the evening event was very well attended by families and friends who shared in the competitive spirit, clearly remembering the winners and their entries year after year."

UPSTAIRS CLASSROOMS

Our school – stories and memories of Bennett Road School, Headingley, 1882–2006

Trips, visits and days out

"I remember the maypole coming out each summer term. A team was picked and rehearsed for weeks prior to the annual Children's Day in Roundhay Park, where schools from all over Leeds would compete in the arena to be city champions (see photo page 26) There was a poster competition in schools to advertise Children's Day every year."

"Mr Hallet, headteacher, was a railway enthusiast and organised a railway circle for any interested pupils. Activities involved visits to places of interest such as Hunslet Engine works, when locomotives were still being made in Leeds."

"I remember Mrs Shuttleworth came from Whitby and was always talking about Whitby and Captain Cook. She took us on trips to Malham Cove and Fountains Abbey."

"The school also entered teams in the Spelling Bee competition. As one of the pupils in the team I enjoyed visiting other schools or entertaining them, when the two panels competed in the word-spelling quiz."

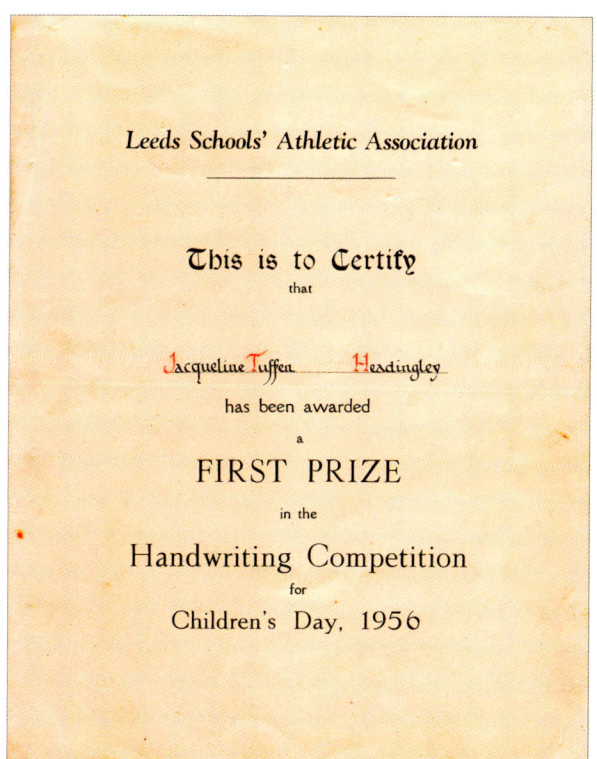

"The school prided itself on its holidays in Europe, instigated I think by Mr Pepper. In my penultimate year we went to Edinburgh and the year after I left I was invited to go to France with school. We stayed in Dieppe (Jean Ango School) with coach trips around Normandy and followed by four nights in Paris."

CHILDREN'S DAY CERTIFICATE
FOR HANDWRITING 1956

DOOR DETAIL

Playtimes

"In the 1950s the traditional old English seasonal past time of conkers were held day after day in the playground. Days of soaking the chestnuts in vinegar at home hardened them for forthcoming contests."

"The school caretaker Mr Bainbridge strictly enforced the rules as to making sure that children didn't venture into prohibited areas and we were more frightened of him than of the teachers."

"Cycling proficiency tests were held in the playground and examiners from ROSPA/CTC came to assess our cycling ability and knowledge of the Highway Code."

In the classroom

"Classrooms still had fireplaces, although not used in my time, as there was central heating. The doors had old-fashioned latches."

School work and ink pens

"One outstanding memory of my first year at Headingley were the desks with ink wells that were full of ink … I had not been introduced to writing with ink or joined up writing at my previous school and here I was landed with having to cope with both.
As a left-hander I always had difficulty in using wet ink (ink wells slotted into holes in desks) without smudging the words I had just written."

"In my first year Mr Hallet (new Head) introduce a "house system" and we wore badges : Green – Bronte House, Red –Priestley, Yellow – Fairfax, and Blue –Delacy. Points were allocated to members of each house for academic work and an element of competition therefore introduced."

The school building

"There were no corridors in the school and so you had to go outside to get from one end of the building to the other. One exception was the very privileged Upper 4 pupil who rang the hand bell at the top of the staircase to mark changes in lesson, as well as playtime, going home time and dinner."

Our school – stories and memories of Bennett Road School, Headingley, 1882–2006

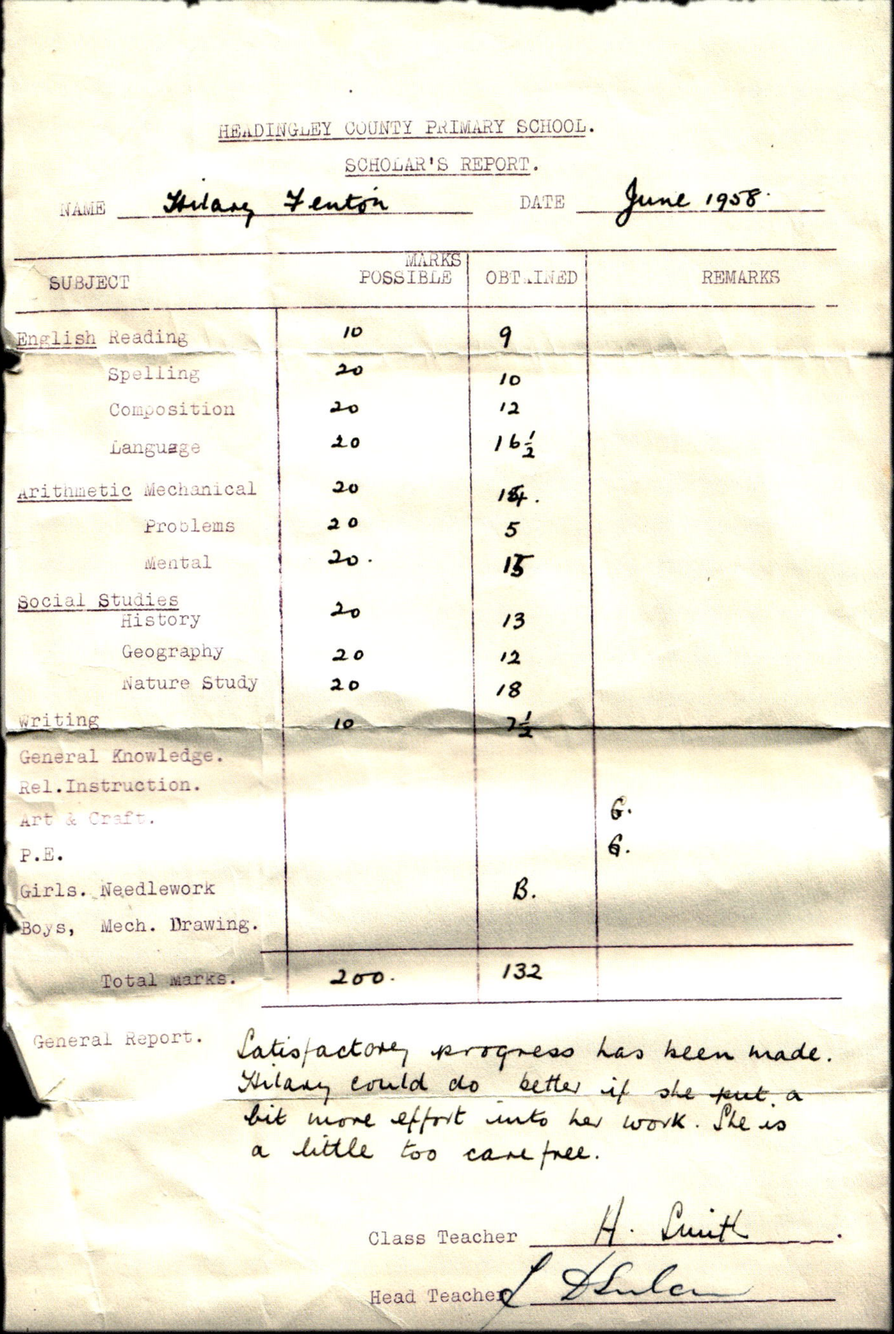

HEADINGLEY COUNTY PRIMARY SCHOOL.

SCHOLAR'S REPORT.

NAME Hilary Fenton   DATE June 1958.

SUBJECT	MARKS POSSIBLE	OBTAINED	REMARKS
English Reading	10	9	
Spelling	20	10	
Composition	20	12	
Language	20	16½	
Arithmetic Mechanical	20	14	
Problems	20	5	
Mental	20	15	
Social Studies History	20	13	
Geography	20	12	
Nature Study	20	18	
Writing	10	7½	
General Knowledge.			
Rel. Instruction.			
Art & Craft.			G.
P.E.			G.
Girls. Needlework			B.
Boys. Mech. Drawing.			
Total marks.	200.	132	

General Report. Satisfactory progress has been made. Hilary could do better if she put a bit more effort into her work. She is a little too carefree.

Class Teacher H. Smith

Head Teacher L. Shula

THE VIEW LOOKING DOWN
THE STAIRS

A bit of ceiling gives way

"In my final year we used a small cloakroom right outside the headmaster's study, which was built, over the west stairwell. The floor consisted of large stone flags one of which was suddenly found to have a chip missing from its corner. For some reason it became the thing to do to put a foot into the space created. I was not the only one to do this but I probably pushed harder and felt the surface below my foot give way. There was a sound like an avalanche and when I went round the top of the stars, I saw a billowing cloud of dust, from which the faces of the people going home peered angrily. These included Mr Coultas (teacher) whose normally ruddy complexion had gone an even deeper shade of purple. Not only was there a pile of plaster on the staircase but part of the wooden cornice had also fallen. Subsequent replastering, and the lack of cornice, was always quite evident on my later visits to the school."

Cricket in the 1950s

"I'm sure the proximity of the county ground had something to do with the fact that all of us boys at Bennett Road seemed to take cricket very seriously too. This was an era, don't forget, in which Yorkshire cricket was extremely successful, extremely good and extremely deep-rooted. So we played cricket a lot. We talked a lot of cricket too, but we played almost as much. We played unsupervised cricket in the boys' playground (the one nearer to Otley Road) at break time and we played supervised cricket in Beckett's Park once a week during 'games'."

"When we batted we had wickets painted on the playground wall and when we bowled we did so from a mound of jumpers and satchels. We had our own rules too – like 'one handed off the wall'. If you hit the ball against the wall and it rebounded to a fielder he had to take it one-handed for the batsmen to be caught. Then there was the batsman's call of 'RST' which meant you were only running to the bowler's wicket and would not go for the return run."

1958 cricket team

"When we played in the park things were more serious. We would walk to Beckett's Park in a supervised column, crossing North Lane by the library (on the corner and now the community centre), going up Ash Road and through the ginnel, two by two, with Mr Sinclair the form master in Upper 4, in charge. There we played on a hard pitch on the top of a rise looking out towards Kirkstall, the pitch covered in matting or rubber, I think, with a harder ball and I think we wore pads when we batted."

"I cant overemphasize how much time we boys (only) spent at break times playing endless cricket! The wickets had been painted on the stonewall and of course only a tennis ball allowed. This was obviously approved of by Mr Sinclair, the teacher who coached the cricket teams. It was quite exciting to visit other schools for away games, improving our geographical knowledge of Leeds."

Other individual memories

"The laundry next door ... I can remember the smell and the clouds of steam now ..."

"I was the only one from the children's home attending the school. It was a friendly school, which helped in me being accepted, and within a short time I had formed friendships."

CLASS PHOTO 1954-5
G.SIDEBOTTOM

6 1960-1990

The three tier school organisation system (with middle schools) began and came to an end in Leeds during this period. Bennett Road had a problem with numbers of classrooms for each year group so the 'one and a half years in each class' idea was developed and seemed to work well. Pupils could be accelerated up into the next class or they could spend longer in one class depending on individual progress and where their friends were.

The school was 100 years old during this time and it seems the famous school song was written by Nancy Beynon as part of the celebrations. (see page 53).

Contributors include: **Jane Bower, Rosie Cantrell, Pat Ledger, Joan March, Rosalyn and Heather Belford, John Munro, Jean Riley, Alistair and Jennifer Stead, Lilian Staton and Jemma Garland.**

Staff recalled: **Mrs Robinson (Head) Mrs Staton, Miss Johnson, Mr Hallet, Mr Penny, Mrs Place, Mrs Nelson, Mrs Shuttleworth, Mrs Smith, Mrs Berry, Mr Sinclair, Mr Coultas, Mrs Haigh, Mrs Howden, Mr Manrai, Mrs Beynon, Mrs O'Neil, Mrs Gravely, Mrs Mayes Mrs Clough, Mrs Howden, Mrs Haigh, Mrs Wells, Mrs Hazlewood, Mrs Garland, Mrs Hepton, (Secretary), Mrs Montague (secretary), Mrs Sharp (caretaker), Mr Milaya (caretaker).**

In the classroom

"Mrs O'Neil's class … at the start of each morning she wrote vast numbers of sums rapidly across the long blackboard in her swift, backward sloping handwriting. She taught us hockey (we had to paint the balls white periodically and dry them on little tripods) and would appear in her white lace-up pumps."

"My first teacher was Mrs Place … we made embroidered doll's blankets, brought items in for the nature table and I remember her saying 'corner to corner and edge to edge' when folding paper."

"We had opening wooden lidded desks with ceramic inkwells inserted in the corners and we wrote with dip pens. My school books show an old fashioned curriculum – dictation, spelling tests, grammar, arithmetical problems about baths filling up at a certain rate!, historical facts – learned by rote."

"We got stars for our work – 10 stars gave you a big silver star on the wall chart and 10 of these gave you a gold! The stars themselves were the reward."

"If you were naughty you would be sent to see Mrs Robinson to explain yourself. Sometimes you might have to face the wall in the corner of the room or stand up with your hands on your head until your arms ached."

"I went into Junior 1 with Miss Johnson – she was a very kind person and made me feel welcome as a new student. I remember sewing things with Binca fabric in her class."

Music

"As I played the violin I was quickly made a member of the school orchestra and I was also in the choir and loved being in concerts, which were regularly performed for parents. Several of my friends also played instruments and we got a lot of encouragement from Mrs Staton (Head) and we were thrilled when she entered us for the Leeds Primary School Orchestra at the Town Hall."

"I remember playing the recorder at Bennett Road and on one occasion the recorder group had rather a difficult tune to play and being the only one able to play it, I was placed by Mrs Staton on a chair (I was about 7 years old) so she could demonstrate how it should be played."

"If you were lucky and if you wanted to you'd be asked to be the person to change the transparencies on the projector in assembly for each song we sung. It was a real privilege to be asked. Similarly, after a music lesson you might be the one to miss part of a lesson so you could dunk all the recorders in disinfectant! Or after art you could clean all the paint pots and brushes out."

School dinners

"School dinners were eaten in the double room downstairs and were horrific to me. I recall truly abominable stews with huge glistening jelly balls of gristle. Also the dreaded custard skin, flopping out of an aluminium jug, lumpy mashed potato and tepid rice pudding with pink, watery jam!"

LEEDS PRIMARY SCHOOLS ROAD SAFETY COMPETITION WINNERS 1980.
BACK ROW: SECOND FROM RIGHT MR PENNNY, FAR RIGHT HEADMISTRESS MRS STATON.
FRONT ROW WINNERS FROM LEFT: ADAM WOODCRAFT, NICHOLA STEAD, SIMON MONTAGUE AND ALAN LACY.

Chapter 6 - 1960-1990

HAND RAIL DETAIL

LEFTHAND DOORWAY AND STONEWORK DETAIL

The school building

"I remember vividly the small fittings and fixtures in the school. The shallow stone steps up to the classrooms, the small intriguing brass studs on the banisters, the thickly painted wooden cupboards, the Bakelite switches and plugs on the walls."

"From the small library room it was possible to see down into the outside boys' toilets. The toilets too were a place of horror. You had to go right outside the school to the back (where the boys were frequently told off for climbing up the coke pile or kicking balls over into the caretaker's garden) and choose an outdoor sandstone cubicle with wooden door and very low children's toilet. In winter huge icicles hung on all the edges of the eaves and we would break them off and yes – suck them!"

"I remember there were very high windows so you couldn't look out, closed doors on separate classrooms … no playing fields nearby … the toilets, outside they froze up in winter … assemblies and PE took place down the road."

"The school building had a ledge about a foot above the ground which it was a challenge to get round, clinging to whatever was there to help balance. There was a high wall round part of the playground too and I was once before the Head for climbing on to that."

The playground

"We all used to get excited on the day of the year that the patterns were painted on the on the playground! I remember the first year of it and wondered why they didn't just give us grass, which would have been much better. However on Sports Day we would always go to St.Michael's on Wood Lane where there was plenty of grass to have races on."

"I spent most playtimes playing French skipping with a loop of elastic or sitting against one of the buttresses jutting out of the front playground wall. We were also allowed round the back where we played skipping using traditional chants."

Headingley Library

"The local library – one of my fondest memories – it was along the street and we were allowed to go there by ourselves – at lunchtime."

Teachers and school staff remembered

"The terrifying infants teacher – Mrs Nelson ... if sent down to her with a message I would stand outside the door for quite a while carefully composing what I had to say – she would jump all over you if she didn't like your manner, grammar, level of politeness etc!"

"Mr Penny, he was a lovely man and he lived with his sister quite near us in Adel. A friend and I went to his house on Mischief night and did spooky things – he was worried that his sister might be frightened."

HEADINGLEY LIBRARY
– LATER HEADINGLEY
COMMUNITY CENTRE

SCHOOL STAFF 1960
HEADTEACHER (MR PENNY
ON THE RIGHT)

Chapter 6 – 1960-1990

LEFT: WHERE THE CARETAKER'S MYSTERIOUS LITTLE DOORWAY WAS – NOW PLASTERED OVER

RIGHT: THE SCHOOL BELL

"I remember one of the teachers gave everyone spanks for their birthday – the number of years you had reached – girls and boys. He was also fond of throwing gym shoes at anyone who wasn't paying attention (others threw chalk)."

"Mrs Montague was the school secretary; she was always walking between classrooms with a green Hessian bag that jangled with coins. Mr Milaya, the caretaker lived behind a secret door at the far end of the playground … where you weren't allowed to go."

"The dinner ladies: Mrs Wells and Mrs Garland, they were lovely but shouted a lot because nobody ever queued in a straight line. They seemed to be in charge of queues, milk and lost property boxes."

Hobbies night

"There was a hobbies night each year, which the 'less crafty' was a bit of a trial. You had to submit a piece of craftwork or something to be judged. If your hobby was ball games or riding your bike and making dens, you were struggling!"

Making the drinks for the teachers

"The prized jobs at school were milk monitor, ringer of the bell and interestingly making the drinks for the teachers at morning break – a particularly popular task it meant leaving lessons a bit early. This was a job for girls in the 1960s and two of us were given the job each day. Inside a cupboard in the staff room was the list of required beverages and we put the kettle on and the milk to boil in a big pan. It was great fun and of course we felt quite important having this job, though nothing could quite match ringing the bell!"

"At some point in your school career, when the middle school system operated in the city, pupils would skip a year or do half a year in one class and half in another."

The school song

"I remember we celebrated the school centenary and the first thing that springs to mind and I still think of whenever I walk past is the school song."

THE SCHOOL SONG
(WRITTEN FOR THE CENTENARY)

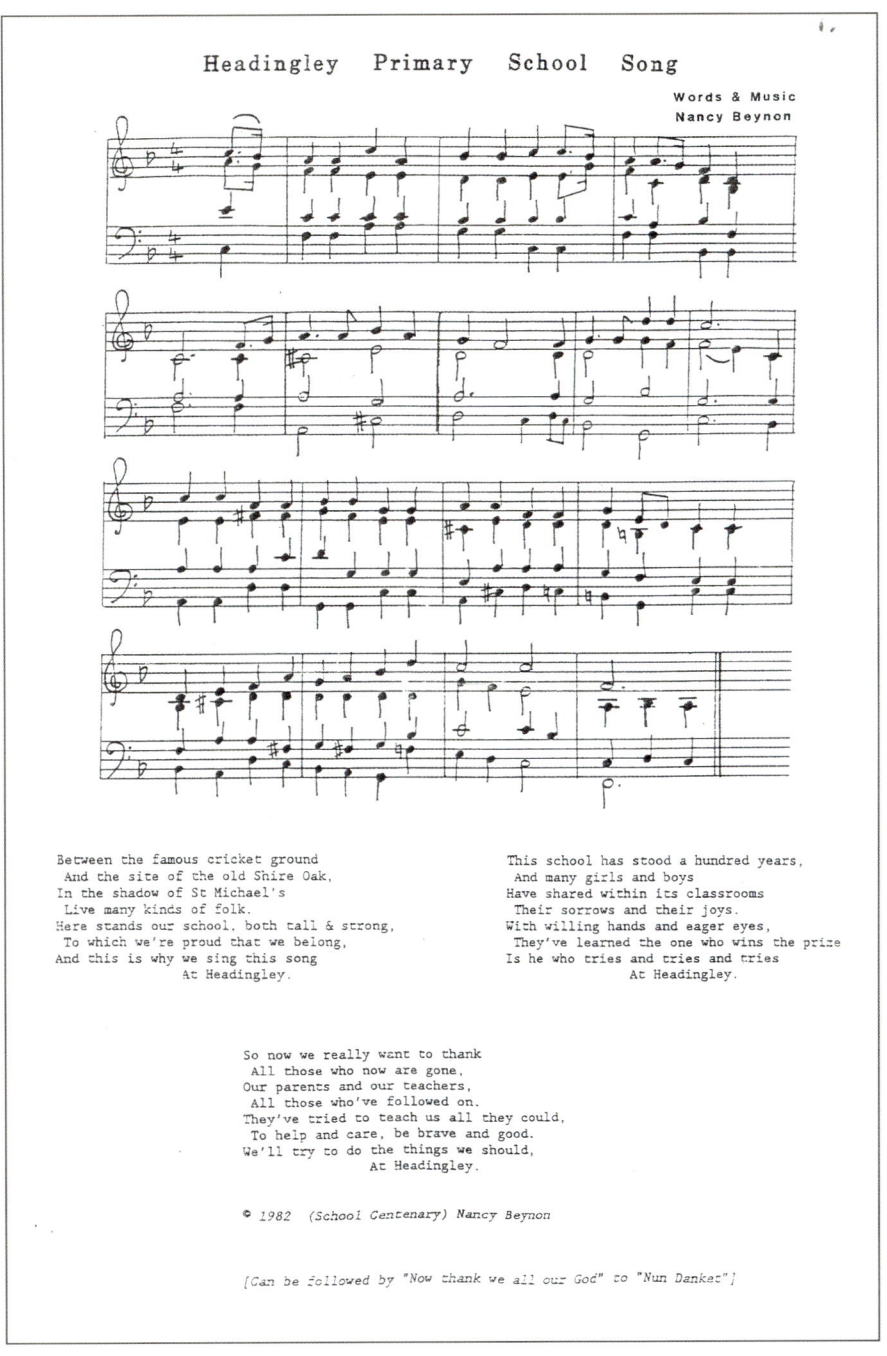

Chapter 6 – 1960-1990

Special visitors

"Instead of a normal assembly of hymns, readings, story or play we sometimes had a special visitor. This might be a policeman or the cycling proficiency man or Wellifant (a big red elephant who told us about the dangers of fire). At Christmas, Santa would come with his sack and every single year we would get a tube of Smarties wrapped up like a cracker in crepe paper and a ribbon!"

"I remember one day making Union Jack hats and flags and going to Otley Road to wave at the Queen as she came past."

School uniform

"I remember I didn't like the bottle green uniform with the logo in a bright ugly yellow!"

MR HALLET AND SCHOOL PREFECTS 1962

Our school – stories and memories of Bennett Road School, Headingley, 1882–2006

YEAR 5 CLASS 1960

7 1990-2006

This period included an excellent time for the school under the charismatic leadership of Mr Sheldrick, who was Headteacher for sixteen years from 1984. The school became very popular and was well known for combining a caring attitude, good standards, excellent results and also great music. (See Yorkshire Evening Post report - page 69). Mr.Sheldrick retired from the school in the summer of 2000 and in the autumn there was a wonderful leaving ceremony for him.

The education authority decided to develop many parts of the school and to replace the temporary classroom (the famous 'Hut') with a stone built permanent classroom. This was something that had been campaigned for over many years. However a few years later came the decision to close the school altogether. There was a closing ceremony in July 2006, bringing to a close 120 years of children's education on the site.

Contributors include: **Elaine Smith, John Sannaee, Jenny Parker, Joan Cunliffe, Alexandra Hurwood, Katie Roche, Rebecca Sells, Ella Jeffries, Sam Webb, Rhiannon Sells, Kate Bavage, Lesley Jeffries and Richard Crossley.**

Staff remembered included: **Mr Sheldrick, Mr O'Grady, Mrs Rix, Mr Kenny and Ms Stevens (Headteachers). Mrs Clough (Deputy Head). Mrs G White, Mrs Mayes, Mrs Cunliffe, Mrs Flanagan, Mrs Parker, Mrs Crook, Mrs Fairclough, Mrs Overend, Mrs Fellows, Mrs P White, Mrs Hall, Mrs Ackroyd (Secretary), Mrs Smith, Mr Lowe (Caretaker).**

Intimate sense of community

"Headingley Primary has left a great impression on me, as I loved my time there, it was a small school and had an intimate sense of community. The teachers and the customs of each year group were all well known to all within the school. I particularly remember our excitement at first getting the chance to learn the recorder in our weekly music lessons, and the genuine horror and fear instilled in us upon being warned never to walk up the stairs with the recorder in our mouths, lest we fall and end up with our recorders impaled through the back of our necks."

"Similarly (though without the fear) it was with great anticipation that we entered the mysterious world of Mrs Clough's 'hut' (the temporary classroom in the playground) on the first day of Class 3/4. Sadly neither Mrs Clough nor the hut are with us any longer, but both will remain linked intrinsically and written indelibly in the minds and memories of the hundreds of children who passed through that class over the years."

"I remember how lucky I felt to be in this grand old institution, which retained its Victorian hearths and the traces of where the old school benches had been stuck into the walls, we had the railings and a playground coloured with netball-pitch lines and colourful animal-shaped re-imaginings of hopscotch and we had split year groups."

LEFT: SCHOOL STAIRCASE

RIGHT: THE TEMPORARY CLASSROOM – THE FAMOUS 'HUT'

Grounded school, good music

"Headingley Primary was a very personable and grounded school with a relaxed and friendly atmosphere, reflected in the optional uniform that hardly anyone wore! The uniform was a green top with the Headingley Primary School logo printed on it – a pair of hands cupping an image of the school building. (see picture) I thought this was very appropriate as I always felt I was in good hands! I have so many fond memories of Headingley Primary School."

"Amongst them is the music we sang: 'When I'm 64' by the Beatles and 'California Dreaming' by the Beach Boys! My favourite song we sang in assembly was 'The Headingley Primary School Song', imprinted in our memory for as long as we shall live! Another favourite was '...the broad beans are sleeping in the blankety bed!' All of which were mimed by me ... apart from when Mr Sheldrick walked round to listen to each of us!"

"Headingley Primary School took great pride in producing musicals at the end of each year such as 'Joseph and the Amazing Technicolor Dream Coat' and 'Bugsy Malone'. These were organised by Mrs Crook our music teacher who always seemed high on life and full of enthusiasm – I only remember her smiling!"

"Around Christmas each year the 'ice rink' would be put down in the assembly hall – it was made up of jigsaw pieces of (plastic) 'ice' – great fun but quite difficult to skate on! For some reason it had a strange smell which would stay in the hall for weeks after!"

"I think the most disappointing thing I can remember about Headingley was the plastic birthday cake they had in reception. On every birthday Mrs Flanigan would appear holding the cake with candles lit and the whole class would sing Happy Birthday, the candles were blown out and then tears of despair would follow when the birthday girl or boy was told they couldn't eat the cake – as it was made of plastic!"

"For me the school was all about friendship and good morals, I still remember Mr Sheldrick telling us a story each day during assembly which had a moral lesson embedded into it – I remember thoroughly enjoying these and I think they have had a lasting impression on me."

The top class

"Perhaps my strongest memories are of Mrs White's class 5/6 where I spent my last two years at Headingley Primary. I remember for the first – and probably the last – time being interested by science lessons; the class hamsters – Nipper and Gnasher; and above all the privileges that came with being the oldest children in the school; sitting on the benches in assembly, ringing the bell to signal the end of school, setting up the 'apparatus' for PE lessons and, in my second year in Mrs White's class, being a 'Golden Oldie', her term for those who spent two years with her as opposed to another class further down the school."

"Even my less positive memories of Headingley are tinged with a sense of fun; our shudders at being forced to drink milk (usually replete with a thick, repellent, layer of curd) became a game of who could get away with drinking the least, sometimes by going so far as to feign sickness; likewise hanging from a bar for what seemed like an eternity whilst dressed as a sloth in the environmentally – aware musical 'Yanomama'– had its reward with the opportunity to sing a solo."

A lively, thriving school

"When I left Headingley, tearfully clutching my dictionary that I was gifted as a memento (as were the other year 6 leavers). I will always remember Headingley Primary as a lively, thriving school where everyone was cared for, everybody knew each other, and the children wanted to learn."

Healthy environment

"My children attended Headingley Primary School during this period and I cannot stress enough how important it was as a start in their lives. They thrived in the caring atmosphere, became both very respectful of and then later healthily sceptical of their teachers. The fact that the school was less than one form entry meant that the classes were all mixed age ranges. I never knew of the children thinking (as we did at that age) that you 'should' only play with your own age group. When my son was in the top year, he spent a lot of time playing with the little ones. This was such a healthy environment for the children."

"I was chair of governors at the time when school budgets were being converted to the one-size-fits-all version whereby the 'money followed the children'. This meant that as a small school, HPS couldn't benefit from the economies of scale that larger schools had. I am proud to say that I (with the support of the governing body) set an 'illegal' budget which was higher than our income! The authorities didn't know how to deal with us!"

The Headteacher

"Mr Sheldrick's gift was his ability to relate to the children whilst still commanding their respect. The funniest moment I remember was when he dressed up as a chicken in yellow fluffy suit for the PTA pantomime. No one knew who the chicken was until the end when he took his bow – and the sight of all those open-mouthed children was wonderful!"

THE GOOSE IN YELOW TIGHTS REVEALED AS HEADTEACHER MR SHELDRICK

The 'Headingley cupboard'

"I don't ever recall thinking that my primary school was small or different from any other school however when I attended high school I remember discovering that it was known by other children as the 'Headingley cupboard' – the tiny hippy school that had too many year groups for the number of classrooms resulting in classes being called 4/5, 5/6 etc ... It was one of the only schools in the area which didn't require the children to wear a uniform! I think it was a brilliant school and remember loving every single teacher!"

The start of school

"The honour of being the bell-ringer! I can see it now ... the big, heavy, bronze old fashioned bell that signalled the start and end of school, playtime and lunchtime!"

Assembly

"The whole school gathered in the school hall. All classes sat cross-legged in rows on the polished wooden floor and then in 5/6 you graduated to sitting on the benches! I remember being given the special task of 'assembly duty' when you were Year 6 and you were allowed to sit on the gym horse at the back of the hall to switch on and off the lights and hold open the doors! I also clearly recall following the pencil pointing out song words on the over-head projector, singing our hearts out in an attempt to impress Mr Sheldrick as he walked past, hand cupped around ear, to inspect our singing abilities ... the school song and many, many Beatle's songs – which are cemented in my memory!"

"Mr Sheldrick used to tell us moral stories and read poems that he loved! I can recall being terrified at the sound of a loud clap and a pointing finger and 'bricks will fall on you boy!!' when somebody was doing something naughty during assembly! To finish assembly, Mr Sheldrick always asked everyone to, 'place your hands together and close your eyes', and said a prayer, 'Dear Father God ... ', even though there was a huge mixture of religions and many atheists!"

SCHOOL STAFF 1987
MR SHELDRICK IN CENTRE

Playtime and lunchtime

"When we used to go into Reception for lunch and we would always ask the dinner lady to 'save us a two-er', or a 'three-er' so we could all sit together!"

"Playtimes – I seem to remember lots of times when someone got stuck in the railings at the front of the school and one particular time the fire brigade being called to get them out!"

"Hours of playing, 'What time is it Mr Wolf?' and then 'The Bill' in older years ... who came up with that name?! 'Wet playtimes', when it rained and we had to stay inside and play the ancient board games that must have been a million years old!"

MRS CUNLIFFE'S CLASS 1991

School milk

"The tiny bottles of milk which Reception and Year 2/3 got and then if there was any leftover got sent to the older years as 'spare milk'!"

"The head-masters office … where Mr Sheldrick and Mrs Ackroyd hid out, (who I used to think were boyfriend and girlfriend!) which you were never allowed in unless showing some work which your teacher had told you was good enough to 'show Mr Sheldrick' and possibly worthy of a sticker! Or if you needed a telling off, Mr Sheldrick had that black book we were threatened with and if you were bad your name went in. I remember you were also allowed in the office to collect the registers which were kept there, this was a job which you could only do in Year 6 and everyone fought for, even though you had to arrive at school early!"

"The music lessons with Mrs Crook … I remember in the earlier years when she was trying to teach us about different sounds and tempos she would bring in those little sock puppets! Three of which I can remember quite distinctly; these were Os.car, Hen.ri.et.ta and Shhheee.ba!?"

PE

"When we played rounder's and everyone wanted to get a 'slogger' out the railings because it meant Mrs White had to run across the road to get the ball and you could get tons of rounder's whilst she attempted to safely but quickly collect the ball in front of a closely watching class!"

Plays

"I also remember clearly the nativity plays we used to do for the parents, the first one was pretty traditional I think and as far as I remember we were all angels and then as the years went on the nativity plays seemed to become a little less traditional as I seem to remember one year being a gannet?! Ha. I also recollect the time one of the teachers set the school staff room on fire by making toast when we were doing a school play and we all had to line up in our costumes outside, that must've looked pretty funny!"

RECEPTION CLASSROOM
1980s

Reception

"I remember a few things from Reception ... like us each having a little picture for our trays and pegs where we used to hang our pump bags on! (Mine was a rose I think!). Also I remember how we all used to stand on the step in reception and wave bye to our mums and dads when they left us for the day, aww. And those word tins we all used to have which were old tobacco tins?! And then at the end of the day we'd have story-time in which loads of us would fall asleep!"

Class 1/2

"Taken by Mrs Fairclough and Mrs Overend who I thought of as twins who took it in turns to take the class … even though they look nothing alike!"

Class 3/4

"'The hut' – I remember a bird flew into the window one day and terrified us and the care-taker nursed it back to health … learning about the Vikings and re-enacting the Viking meal eating nettle tops and elderflower juice … don't remember much else other than the nice food to be honest. Mrs Clough with her polo mints for good behaviour!"

MRS MAYES' CLASS

Class 5/6

"The merit box(a plastic tub!), everytime we were good we'd get merits (small plastic cubes), and when we were naughty e.g., if we wouldn't stop talking, Mrs White would stand at the front of the class and start removing merits from the merit box. If we had enough as a class by Friday afternoon we'd get an extra half hour play-time! Mrs White, amazing teacher (Year 5/6 teacher)who occasionally brought her sheep in to school and always had a saddle on the back seat of her car! I remember she made us all conquer our fears of public speaking by standing on 'the box' at the front of the classroom and giving a talk on something interesting!"

"It is amazing how vivid some memories are. The progression from cheekily peering behind the piano at my fellow wrong-doer whilst being punished on the rug-covered steps in Reception Class, all the way to becoming one of Mrs White's 'Golden Oldies' in Year 6 is filled with quite a few of them, albeit with quite a few gaps."

"The fake birthday cake ... As I recall it was brought out in Reception for every child's birthday. The eternal disappointment of it not being a real cake was only slightly assuaged by the bright blue lining, glistening (if pretend), the candles and the fact that it did look pretty tasty."

Chess

"Chess will always be a lasting memory from HPS. Mr Sheldrick taking on five or six kids at a time at chess club served to create the most competitive seven year old chess players you'll ever see. I distinctly remember the amazing mix of jealousy, resentment, wonder and admiration felt towards anyone who beat him. I suppose, not being able to remember if I ever beat him, would suggest that I never did. However, our chess tours to other schools were fun. I remember being placed on a low down ranking on a game against another school only to not only win my game but to then go on to defeat the 3rd seeded opposition player in a friendly after the tournament. Probably the highest sporting achievement of my life."

Bugsy Malone

"The shows that school put on were always pretty incredible. I can now only recall two of them whilst I was there. However, any HPS aficionado would surely admit that Bugsy Malone was a creative masterpiece. From the immense (or what seemed immense to an 11 year old) tripped-out city backdrop, through the incredible dance scenes all the way to the ridiculously oversized costumes, it was incredible. An all-round success in every conceivable way."

Assembly

"An aphoristic man, Mr Sheldrick would use assemblies to regale us with numerous stories, biblical anecdotes and moral teachings. Similarly he had a few neat phrases that were to be used in case of a disruption. His favorite simile to be used to intervene in such disruptions was the infamous "If you don't behave sonny, I will come down on you like a ton of bricks!". Of course the assemblies held another joyous memory, the school song. This I'm sure I can remember and I could probably recite the whole first verse even now:

"Beneath the famous cricket ground in the shade of the old Shire Oak ..."

(See page 53 for all the words ... and music!)

"Memories of assemblies, and of course the school song, also include the great Mrs Crook, the music teacher. Her cheerful bashing away at the piano in the school hall will always stay with me. She started so many of us off with a great love of music and her enthusiasm was fairly infectious."

Playground games

"The Bill: finally there was the catch-them-chase-them game that was inexplicably called 'the Bill'. Using the steps up to 'the hut' as the prison (which I guess actually might explain the game's name) and the steps up the far end of the building as a safe zone a normal game of 'tig' would commence. However, somehow the rules came to allow that the 'prisoners' would be able to make a chain to get tagged free. If there was enough people it was possible to create a chain that could reach all the way to the safe base thereby ensuring freedom and much hilarity – a feat worthy of celebration."

BUGSY MALONE
PROGRAMME

Music

"I always enjoyed the musical aspects of my time at Headingley Primary. From singing in assembly (although I never actually admitted this to my friends) to composing 'raps' in Mrs Crook's music lessons and then there were the school plays ... my favourite role would have to be playing a sloth in 'Yanomano' although I had originally wanted to be a jaguar. I got to sing a solo and think I drove my family mad by practising at home all the time! Also the pantomime that the teachers and parents put on was pretty unforgettable, especially when I found out that it was Mr Sheldrick that had been hiding in that chicken suit the whole time, I could not stop laughing, I thought it was absolutely brilliant!"

Learning

"On the academic side of things I remember loving my spelling tin and meticulously learning every single word written on coloured paper that I had tipped out on to the carpet at home, only putting the word back in the tin when I had definitely grasped its spelling. Also I remember Mr Sheldrick's handwriting lessons, they were always a scary affair, 'a t should be the size of a capital letter' and so forth. Probably the best poetry I have written was produced in Mrs Cunliffe's class in 2/3, I can still recite my proudest creative pieces to this day."

MRS FLANAGAN AND RECEPTION CLASS 1994

"I think what made Headingley special was the close-knit environment that the small school, mixing of year groups and personal approach of the teachers created. Mind you the teachers were definitely all unique and there was a certain mystique surrounding each one and their reputation, so that you heard from the older years what it would be like to be in each class and in a way, you always wanted to move up the school to experience the next one."

School tables rebel comes out top

BY MIKE HURST

THE top-scoring Leeds school in league tables published today had boycotted the exercise, labelling it unfair and inaccurate.

The Government published performance tables for every primary school in England, comparing results in last year's tests and teacher assessments for 11-year-olds in English, maths and science.

The top schools in Leeds were Headingley Primary and St Peter and St Paul's Primary schools at Yeadon which both scored 282. The national average was 170.7.

But Headingley did not submit the teacher assessment scores, in protest at what the governors said was a system which unfairly damns some schools while praising others.

The stance was criticised today by Education Secretary Gillian Shephard.

She said: "A small minority of schools refused to send in their teacher assessment marks. This is frankly shameful and insulting to the parents and communities they should be serving."

Reflect

But Headingley head teacher Frank Sheldrick said: "We didn't send in our teacher assessments because we didn't feel the system was fair. Our governors felt the system of testing does not really reflect on the hard work and dedication put in by hundreds of primary teachers across the Leeds authority."

Mr Sheldrick added: "I am very pleased that we have done so well because it underlines all the hard work of staff and children and the high level of support we get from parents."

YORKSHIRE EVENING POST ARTICLE

The Pantos

I still remember the audible gasp from pupils and their family and friends when the identity of the star of the show – a large goose in fetching bright yellow tights – was revealed to be none other than head-teacher Mr Sheldrick. This was at the end of Mother Goose, a pantomime written, produced, directed and performed by parents and staff from the school. With a live band including pupils as well as parents, the talented and not-so-talented-but-willing took to the stage in January 1998, surprising the audience (and possibly themselves) with their memorable performances.

LEFT: MOTHER GOOSE

RIGHT: TWO SCENES FROM ALADDIN

Finally, we have collected together some brief snippets of memories mentioned on Facebook. There are over 100 ex-pupils on the Facebook Headingley Primary School group. This is a sample from recent pupils:

The Headteacher

"My favorite Sheldrick-ism is 'I will come down on you like a ton of bricks!' – what a guy!"

"... well my favorite Sheldrick-ism was 'can you see the steam coming out of my ears!?'"

"... the best ever was the 'you're skating on thin ice, boy ... don' t be the second person to fall in'."

"Mr Sheldrick the headteacher – I remember him telling us a story about a dragon and this boy, and he'd carry on this story every time we had a lesson with him and the story went on for over a year ... but basically this dragon and this little boy ..."

The school song

"Best song was the Headingley primary school song 'Beeeeneath the famous cricket ground, in the sight of the old shire oak, in the shaaadow of St.Michael's live many kinds of folk'."

"... between the famous cricket ground and the site of the old shire oak. Yeah I remember that ..."

Year 6 privileges

"Gutted that when I got to Year 6 the new headteacher decided it was too dangerous for us to sit on benches in assembly – I couldn't believe it! my entire schooling career had been leading up to that privilege!"

The staff room fire

"I do remember the fire, (the toaster in the staff room started it!) everyone being told to stand around the hut and various people crying. The smell afterwards was pretty bad – class 5/6 was right next to the staff room and we had to put up with it for weeks before they found some fresh paint ... and a new toaster."

8 HEART – a new era

By 2006 it had been decided to close the school – it seemed as if numbers had dropped in the area and a plan to combine St Michael's and Bennett Road schools was eventually agreed. St Michael's had a more attractive site with much more space for buildings – and green space around it. The combined school has been given a new name the 'Shire Oak School' following a parental vote. Many of the staff from Bennett Road also went on to the new combined school.

In July 2006 there was a sad but wonderful closing ceremony where many people came and shared their memories of happy times over the years at the school.

What would happen to the building then became a most important question – could it be saved from being converted into yet more Headingley living accommodation ... or worse? An exciting and daring scheme began to be plotted within and around the Headingley Development Trust using the building as the base for a combined local arts / business / community. After an incredibly hard fought campaign LCC eventually agreed to the ambitious and forward looking scheme.

A superbly imaginative design was created and the new look building is being refurbished as we complete this booklet. The design has cleverly retained many original features – the outside is mainly as it was with a new entrance in the centre. The inside has been opened up including a mezzanine floor in the open roof space! Many features which had been covered up for years and years have been unearthed and set to prominence within the new internal design.

HEART (Headingley Enterprise and Arts Centre) will be opening early in 2011 and so the building will continue to serve the local community albeit in a new and exiting way, continuing its 120 years of fascinating history.

HEART UNDER CONSTRUCTION

The collection goes on growing

If you would like to either know more or indeed to contribute to the collection of memories and you have access the internet then please go to www. headingley.org where you will be able to see more of the original text and have the opportunity to add you own memories – we hope that you will!

We hope that it may also be possible to add written memories via a collection point at the old school itself, after it opens as HEART in early 2011.

References and acknowledgements

We are grateful to the West Yorks Archive service for permission to reproduce documents:

LC/ED/acc3204/73 Headingley school building plans drawn 1880

LC/ED/WYAS1821/plan84 Headingley P school building plans, 19th century

LC/ED216/box2/WYAS3068 log book 1905-1937

LC/ED216/box1/WYAS3068 Log book 1937-1972

LC/ED216/WYAS3068/box1/Log book Infants 1882-1903

C/ED216/WYAS3068 /box2/Log book Girls 1882-1905

C/ED216/WYAS3068/box4/ Admissions register 1924-40

C/ED216/WYAS3068/box2/ Punishment book 1905-66

To Leodis website for permission to reproduce photographs:

Copyright Leodis Library and Information Service – www.Leodis.net

To Yorkshire Post, permission to reproduce photographs:

Picture courtesy of Yorkshire Post Newspaper

Design: dg3 design – www.dg3.co.uk

Index

A

Ackroyd, Miss	15
Ackroyd, Mrs	56, 63
Air raid shelter	32
Aladin	70
Arithmetic	16, 29
Assembly	62, 67

B

Bailey, Miss	15
Bainbridge, Mr	44
Beckett's Park	18, 19, 23, 32, 37, 46, 47
Bennett Road	1, 2, 6, 13, 15, 16, 23, 27, 30, 31, 32, 33, 34, 37, 38, 46, 48, 49, 70, 72
Bennett Road/Headingley Primary	13
Berry, Mrs	48
Beynon, Mrs	48
Bloomfield, Miss	22
Booth, Mr	15
Boyle, Miss	8
Bronte	44
Bronwich, Miss	34
Bugsy Malone	58, 66, 75
Bullimore, Miss	22
Burrell, Miss	15, 22, 34

C

Calvert, Miss	15, 20
Cane	28, 41
Cardigan Estate	6
Chess	66
Children's day	26
Children's Day	20, 26, 37, 43
Christmas	30, 54
Classroom	7, 12, 16, 17, 24, 28, 32, 34, 36, 42, 44, 48, 56, 57, 64, 66
Classroom life	28
Classrooms	16, 44
Clough, Mrs	48, 56, 57, 65
Cole, Miss	15, 22, 31
Composition	29
Conkers	27, 44
Corporal punishment	12, 41
Coultas, Mr	46, 48
Cricket	26, 31, 37, 46, 47, 67, 71
Cripps, Mr	15
Crook, Mrs	56, 63, 67, 68
Culture	37
Cunliffe, Mrs	56, 68
Cycling proficiency	44

D

Day, Miss	22, 34, 38
Dean, Mr	15
Delacy	44
Dentist	30
Dictation	48
Downing, Miss	15, 22, 32, 34

E

Early history	4
Education Act, 1944	13, 34
Electric tram	18, 25

F

Fairclough, Mrs	56, 65
Fairfax	44
Fellows, Mrs	56
Flanagan, Mrs	56, 58
France	37, 43
French skipping	50

G

Games	18, 23, 26, 27, 30, 46, 47, 52, 62, 67
Garland, Mrs	48, 52
Gas masks	32
Geography	30
Governors	60
Grammar	48, 51
Grant, Miss	29
Gravely, Mrs	48
Gray Trophy	37
Gregson, Miss	15, 22

H

Haigh, Mrs	48
Hallet, Mr	40, 43, 44, 48
Handwriting Competition	26
Hazlewood, Mrs	48, 52
Headingley Board School	4
Headingley County Primary	13, 38
Headingley cupboard	61
Headingley Development Trust	72
Headingley Primary	1, 2, 13, 57, 58, 60, 68, 75, 76
Headteacher	8, 19, 20, 22, 24, 25, 29, 37, 43, 51, 61, 71
Heal, Miss	22
HEART	3, 72, 73
Hepton, Mrs	48
History	30
Hobbies	42, 52
Horse-drawn tram	4
Howden, Mrs	48
Hut	56, 57, 65, 67, 71

I

Infants' School	8
Ink monitor	25
Ink pens	44
Iron railings	16, 23

J

Johnson, Miss	34, 48, 49
Joseph and the Amazing Technicolor Dream Coat	58

K

Keeping order	12
Kelly, Miss	15
Kenny, Mr	56

L

Laundry	17, 47
Leeds Primary School Orchestra	49
Leeds Schools Athletic Association	20
Lessons	9, 16, 17, 23, 24, 29, 42, 53, 57, 60, 63, 68
Lister, Mr	15
Literature	16
Longstaff, Mr	34
Lunchtime	30, 32, 34, 36, 51, 62

M

Mahoney, Mr	34
Manrai, Mr	48
Matthews, Miss	22, 34, 38
Mayes, Mrs	56, 65
McCann, Mr	34, 37
Merit box	66
Milaya, Mr	52
Milk monitor	41, 53
Montague, Mrs	52
Morley, Mr	15, 19
Mother Goose	70
Music	49, 68

N

National School	7
Nature Study	29
Needlework	9, 29
Nelson, Mrs	34, 48, 51
Noel, Mr	56

O

Off-site visits	19
O'Grady, Mr	56
O'Neil, Mrs	48
Original oak	18
Overend, Mrs	56, 65

P

Painting Lesson	29
Pantos	70
Parker, Mrs	56
Parochial Church Hall	23, 31
Parochial Institute	6, 34, 41
PE	16, 23, 34, 50, 60, 64
Pearsall, Miss	34
Penny, Mr	48, 51
Pepper, Mr	34, 36, 37, 40, 41, 43
Pilling, Miss	15, 22, 31
Place, Mrs	48
Playground	6, 8, 10, 16, 18, 23, 27, 30, 31, 34, 37, 44, 46, 50, 52, 57
Plays	64
Playtime	18, 23, 37, 38, 44, 62
Poetry	29
Poll, Mr	15
Practical skills	29
Priestley	44
Punishment Book	11, 12

R

Reading	16

Reception	64, 66	Staton, Mrs	34, 48, 49
Richard Adams	6	Stevens, Ms	56
Rix, Mrs	56	St. Michael's Church	31, 33
Robinson, Mrs	48, 49	Story time	30
Roundhay Park	26, 43	Subjects studied	29
Rugby	31, 41	Sweet shop	28
Rugby League	18, 41	Swimming	24

S

School bell	52
School Board	6
School building	2, 6, 15, 23, 24, 34, 44, 50, 74
School day	15, 16, 24, 36, 41
School dinners	49
School Log Book	9
School milk	63
School organisation	15
School report	45
School song	48, 53, 62, 67, 71
School uniform	54
Second World War	3, 22, 23, 25, 27, 29, 31, 33, 34
Sharp, Mrs	48
Sheldrick, Mr	56, 58, 61, 62, 63, 66, 67, 68, 70, 71
Shuttleworth, Mrs	43, 48
Sinclair, Mr	34, 41, 47, 48
Singing	29
Site and Building	6
Smith, Mrs	48, 56
Spelling	43, 48, 68
Spelling Bee	43
Sports Day	23, 50
Stars	24, 46, 49

T

The 11+	36
The Bill	62, 67
Thomson, Miss	34
Townson, Mrs	34
Travel	30
Trips	19, 37, 43

W

Wells, Mrs	52
White, Mrs	56, 60, 64, 66
Wilkinson, Miss	14

Y

Yorkshire Penny Bank	30